FOUR STUDIES IN LOYALTY

Hailed as a classic when first published in 1946, *Four Studies in Loyalty* is reprinted here with a new introduction by David Pryce-Jones. This extraordinary collection of essays, each on a different aspect of loyalty, begins with an account of the author's uncle, and his strange and enduring friendship with Edward, Prince of Wales. The second essay tells of the eccentric Persian, Bahram Kirmani, and his unswerving loyalty to Oxford University—a place of learning he never actually attended. The third considers Robert Byron's loyalty to his art, in particular the art of travel writing; and the fourth deals with the loyalty of a band of French men and women to England as witnessed in the Vozges, behind German lines, in the closing years of the Second World War.

David Pryce-Jones, novelist, biographer and travel writer, was literary editor for *Time and Tide* and the *Spectator* before turning to freelance writing. His publications include *Next Generation*, *Owls and Satyrs*, *Evelyn Waugh and his World* (ed), *The Face of Defeat*, *Unity Mitford: a Quest* and the acclaimed biography of Cyril Connolly. His next novel, *Face to Face*, is to be published by Weidenfeld & Nicolson in 1986.

D1149737

FOUR STUDIES IN LOYALTY

Christopher Sykes

INTRODUCTION BY
David Pryce-Jones

CENTURY HUTCHINSON LTD
LONDON   MELBOURNE   AUCKLAND   JOHANNESBURG

To
Diane Abdy

First published in 1946 by William Collins & Sons Co Ltd
Reprinted 1947

© Christopher Sykes 1946
© Introduction David Pryce-Jones 1986

This edition first published in 1986 by Century Hutchinson Ltd,
Brookmount House, 62–65 Chandos Place, London, WC2N 4NW

Century Hutchinson Publishing Group (Australia) Pty Ltd
PO Box 496, 16–22 Church Street, Hawthorn, Melbourne, Victoria 3122

Century Hutchinson Group (NZ) Ltd
PO Box 40-086, 32–34 View Road, Glenfield, Auckland 10

Century Hutchinson Group (SA) Pty Ltd
PO Box 337, Berglvei 2012, South Africa

Printed and bound in Great Britain by
Richard Clay (The Chaucer Press) Ltd,
Bungay, Suffolk

ISBN 0 7126 9458 7

INTRODUCTION

LOYALTY CAN BE to a friend, a place, an ideal, and each expression of it is attractive. Everyone includes loyalty on the secret list of their virtues, and hopes that the word will feature in what others say about them. Actual expressions of loyalty are variously given by Christopher Sykes in this all-too-short book, but its fame and resonance have derived from something wider: loyalty in the sense of being true—being true to oneself and to the world. When this book was first published, such loyalty had been under strain, as it continues to be, for that matter.

Only a small part of *Four Studies in Loyalty* deals directly with the war against Nazism. Remarks here and there reveal that Christopher Sykes had served in the Middle East and afterwards parachuted into occupied France, but personal bravery and all that is somehow to be taken for granted. The people he chose to celebrate are his own long-dead uncle; a former travelling companion, Robert Byron; and endearing or unusual foreigners, Persian or French, who, when put to the test, showed that particular loyalties could also be universal.

Whatever else it is, the English character has always been loyal to itself, and in a thousand years the Nazis could never have acquired a sound sense of it—that baffling thing of mood and style and timing which brought about their un-doing, and is so perfectly expressed in the approach of this book to its subjects. One likes to visualise idealogues reading the story of the author's uncle, for example, another Christopher Sykes. The poor fellow put his trust in princes—or, rather, one prince, the future King Edward VIII—and was ruined by it. But *lèse-majesté* or republican morality does not raise an ugly head. The Snob and the Vulgar Royal Party had simply played out allotted roles in the grand comedy of English life, and not for a moment would either have wished it otherwise.

Humorous appreciation of these matters goes with free-born confidence. Here our author was fortunate in that his father was Sir Mark Sykes of Sledmere, Yorkshire land-owner and baronet, linguist and politician; unfortunate, in that he was a younger son, that peculiar social category deriving from primogeniture, and as English as cheddar cheese.

Younger sons in a family like that are equipped at Eton and Oxford for a position which they do not inherit, obliged to respond to the idea of individual worth, meaning in practice that they survive as rolling-stones. What would literature or adventure be without younger sons? True to form, in the '30s Christopher Sykes was to be found in faraway places, learning languages and writing as he pleased.

Robert Byron, with whom he went to Persia, Afghanistan and India, was another of the same kind; penniless bearer of a famous name. The portrait drawn of him is a lucid little masterpiece, altogether a key to understanding the times. Superficially Byron might have appeared an opinionated Oxford aesthete, accustomed to having his own way, in the manner of those who in a famous debate at the Oxford Union voted not to fight for King and country. Instead, intelligence and experience told him that Nazism would have to be fought, and he has the honour of belonging to the tiny circle of those who gave the warning well in advance, and in a tone of voice to break through complacency. The classic scene in which he leaned across a table to ask an appeaser, "Are you in Germany pay?" continues to give pleasure and comfort.

Quite how public opinion comes to be formed is beyond charting, but Robert Byron had a clear-sightedness which spread further than his social circle. Another contemporary, George Orwell, reached similar conclusions, and there is much to compare and contrast in this apparently unlikely pair. Both took pains to teach themselves to write with clarity, and were indifferent to fashion or popularity in what they then wrote. Their premature deaths (in 1941 Byron was on a ship torpedoed without survivors) have left question-marks about the books they might have written. Robert Byron was cosmopolitan where Orwell was more narrow and political, but a case can be made that in the years leading to the war their different efforts above all made for steadiness among the thinking classes, ever prone to wobble.

"Imagine myself", Sykes writes, "a tall, very young Englishman, and the little round partridge-like figure waddling by my side, pointing his clouded cane in different directions as we walked through the huge piazza or mingled in the crowds and din of the domed bazaars." The imagining is easy. The tradition is the familiar one of a Western visitor and his local guide, in this instance one Bahram Kirmani, in Isfahan. The portrait sounds almost blatant: Bahram too evidently a rogue and fantasist, with his high tales of St Petersburg and Oxford and his low life as pimp and drunkard. A role has chosen him rather than he choosing it. Yet the comic is not to be separated from the all-too-deadly-serious when Bahram rejects the offer to work as agent or informer for the Germany consul in war-time Tehran with the words, "I am surprised that you are so foolish as to make such a suggestion to a Balliol man."

It is fine and proper to have the final essay about the courageous men and women whom Christopher Sykes encountered in the Vozges on his military mission to the Resistance. At the time of writing, he could hardly have been expected to stand back for the sake of objectivity. But the danger to the Resistance and its sympathisers, we now perceive, lay less in the occupying German army than in other Frenchmen, collaborators and *miliciens*, who owed a considerable proportion of their successes, what is more, to anonymous denunciations.

Love of the grand gesture, of colour and heroism, in the fact of an instinct that the sublime and the ridiculous are as siamese twins—the enemies of England have never been able to sort it out. As for us, and our friends, we keep the record through books like this one; and cherish it.

David Pryce-Jones
1986

FOREWORD

IN THE GROUPING of these studies I have been guided by a chronological sequence beginning outside the present century and continuing through personal experience. I have not stressed the connection in time between my first and second subjects, as I am uncertain of the degree of its strength. When I once asked Bahram whether he had ever met my great-uncle, he replied that he had frequently made his acquaintance "in royal circles so-called," but as he never elaborated on this acquaintance, or referred to it again, I take it that what meeting occurred was not of a very material kind. But beyond doubt they shared the same world of pomp and pleasure for a brief space. Between my second and third subjects the link is plain: in the best book he lived to write, Robert Byron was reaping where Bahram in his queer fashion had sown. They were both Oxonians in differing degrees, though Robert never looked back to the University with the affection whose glow coloured Bahram's whole existence. I remember both as companions of unforgettable Persian travels. Between Robert Byron and the experiences I record in my last study, I trust that I have plainly implied another link: the resurrection of France in the war was the answer to consistent faith in Europe such as he had.

My original plan was to compose my book of three studies of individual character followed by a study of group character—the character of a town. Though this intention did not signify any predilection on my part for the hive aspect of human affairs (on the contrary, I remain an unrepentant individualist), I do believe—indeed I have no alternative—that circumstances can call forth, how lastingly it would be hard to say, great manifestations of common character as marvellous or as terrible as the fullest flowering of an individual identity. I suppose that the mass-degradation of the citizens of modern totalitarian states presents the most arresting example of this fact in its evil aspect which can be found in the whole history of the world. What is less easily noted, though future experience may make it common-place, is the strength of the response to this challenge. It is easier to believe in vileness than virtue. I have asked the reader to believe that the evil mass-character of the Germans was surpassed in strength by the opposing mass-character of the French. I saw this living thing in action in a French town, and I determined as a mark of gratitude, to attempt to depict in words the single character which then animated those many souls.

I must own that I found this task beyond me, and finally abandoned it for the less ambitious essay which I present in this book. I present instead a gallery of portraits of French men and women whom I met in those times of stress, hoping that the cumulative effect may convey some impression of that now extinct mass-impulse of France to which so many of us owe our lives. There is no fiction in this book, though in the last essay, as, for obvious reasons, in one or two other places, I have suppressed or altered some names.

Having said thus much about the aim and design of this book, I would like to add a further note on the subject of my principal essay: Robert Byron. Uncertain as such things must be, I have little doubt that had he lived he would have become one of the great names of our time. As it is, the early interruption of his achievement is likely to restrict his memory to the lifetime of his friends. Much would be lost if that should happen. I hope that at some future date it may be possible to produce a full-length book on him. I should like to see such a book written by many hands in the style of that remarkable experiment in biography, *T. E. Lawrence, by his Friends*. I see no reason why such a book should not be as successful in dealing with a relatively obscure subject as it was in dealing with one so famous. If in the meantime my present sketch can do a little to rescue the name of that beloved friend from oblivion, these studies in loyalty will have served purpose enough.

MAY, 1946.   C.S.

I

BEHIND THE TABLET

"So, Uncle, there you are."—HAMLET.

I LIKE to reflect that my name may be immortal; that though it may be forgotten before Shakespeare's sonnets are, it will live as long as certain monuments of Princes. It is inscribed on a tablet over the portal of a renowned royal chapel. If you read the legend, you may learn that a man bearing the same Christian and surnames as myself was for many years the friend of the Prince with whose name the chapel is so intimately connected; that he often worshipped God in this same temple in company with this Prince; that the Prince in memory of his greatly valued friend erected this tablet; and so on. It runs for about eight lines. Well, that is not an immortality to run very far against powerful rhyme, but it is better than nothing, and I am sure that my uncle, Christopher Sykes, would have been very touched and grateful. It is his reward. He liked fame, and fame in this form would have suited his taste very well. I am glad that he did get something out of his long career of painful, of agonising devotion. Many hundreds of visitors to the chapel must see the tablet every year, and I suppose a few score of them trouble to read the legend over the rich Gothic porch, and of these last a few may pause at a dim evocation of some noble companionship of yore. None of them, I feel sure, guess at the apalling story which lies behind the simple words.

The story begins a long way away both in place and time from the holy vulgarities of the royal chapel. It begins, roughly speaking, in the latter half of the eighteenth century on the chill wolds of East Yorkshire, in the house of Christopher's father.

It is a weakness of our imagination, a constant falsification of understanding by the artistry of memory, that we so easily think of the past in terms of its most exquisite masterpieces. Fielding showed us of what raw savage stuff eighteenth-century life in England was made, but we persist in imagining that ferocious epoch as one enormous picture by Sir Joshua Reynolds, a limitless minuet, a dream of colonnades, porticoes, and classical palaces. I doubt whether its most probable virtues, its stability and harmony, the "sweetness of life" extolled (in old age) by Talleyrand, existed at all noticeably outside small choice circles. In the person of my hero's father the eighteenth century lived long into the nineteenth on those then remote uplands, and the last glimpse of the age of reason which men had through him did not recall Lord Chesterfield so forcibly as Squire Western.

He was famous in his day. In such centres of sporting culture as Yorkshire, Melton Mowbray, and Newmarket, he is not quite forgotten even now. He was called Sir Tatton Sykes. Frequent references to this baronet occur in the novels of Surtees, in which he figures generally as "old Tat," also as "Sir Tat," and "Tatters"; and I have noticed that it is often difficult to determine whether he is treated as a figure of fun or veneration in those splendid romances. Possibly as both. He lived to extreme old age, being born before the Duke of Wellington and not dying till the eighteen sixties. From youth to death he never weakened in an almost insane passion for fox-hunting, racing, and the very companionship of horses. It formed the whole basis of his life and character. He never sold a horse if he could avoid doing so, and yet, oddly enough, he parted at a cheap price with the best and most famous of his breed. Taking Surtees as my authority once more, I find myself in doubt as to whether he was looked on as an astute or a poor judge of the animal he so madly worshipped.

As might be expected, he was an eccentric. Until his death in the age of peg-top trousers he wore the long high-collared coat of the regency, chokers, frills, and mahogany topped boots. He was very vain, he exploited the then meagre arts of publicity with shrewdness. His engraved picture and later his daguerreotype, taken in the act of patting or, as portrayed by Sir Francis Grant, riding one of his numerous favourite horses, or reposing in his boots after hunting, with a smile on his countenance fairly bursting with benevolence and cunning, these likenesses were widely circulated among sportsmen of the time. Ludicrous and yet respected, a charlatan in some ways, and yet a homely, comforting, familiar figure, a symbol and a caricature of England, I dare say he was revered and mocked in equal degrees. He was much loved too. To the credit of our humanity, the last departing tenants of an age received an affectionate farewell as a rule. "Tat" was almost the last human being of the eighteenth century to leave the world and his fellow-men honoured him greatly for it. But they would have honoured him a little less, I feel, if they had known how he preserved to the last the more revolting vices of the brutal age which produced him.

His pleasant Adamesque house was a barbaric hell. He ruled over his family with the vicious rage of a stone-age tyrant. That fierce and obscure revival of parental oppression which, according to its historian, Samuel Butler, first became noticeable in the mid-eighteenth century and did not decline till some eighty or ninety years later, this extraordinary relapse found absolute personification in the home life of the old sportsman. He begot a large family: two sons and six daughters. On them he imposed simple and intolerable rules of life: that the virtues resided in rising at dawn in Winter and Summer, on no hot water, on no creature comforts (the girls slept in one small room), and on submission to frequent applications of the paternal whip. An enigmatical portrait survives of his wife, painted by Sir Francis

Grant. Resignation and hardness are oddly combined in her features; one wonders whether she made this bestial manner of life less unbearable for her children. There are traditions that in Yorkshire she was of no account in the house, but that in London, where she was a hostess of fashion, Tatton went in considerable awe of her. As the children spent most of their life in Yorkshire, it may be taken as fairly certain that, even if she possessed a kind heart, which I doubt, their sufferings were little mitigated; and with increasing age the old tyrant relinquished none of his heavy rule.

When his sons returned from the squalor of school they were often greeted with flagellations which must have made them sigh for the birches of Harrow; on one occasion the discipline was administered because, on unpacking, the unmanly frippery of tooth-brushes was discovered among their effects. The elder boy, being the weaker of the two, was treated with a special concern. The heroic old father was once seen armed with a whip driving the child barefoot and screaming down the drive. It is not surprising that normal growth was contorted on this poisonous ground. That the two boys should have grown up to detest their father was natural and even proper. What I find interesting is the extraordinary divergence in character, divergence both in protest from the paternal type and from one another, which their later history manifested. The elder son, Tatton, turned into a sensitive, bitter, eccentric, loveless man. What the younger son Christopher became it is my purpose to show.

One thing only did the two brothers have in common. The forms of escape which they chose were in both cases profoundly romantic. The second Tatton put himself at the greatest possible distance from the world; he sought consolation in Oriental travel, in building quantities of Gothic churches, in solitude. His strange character was strangest in the conjunction of a harsh aptitude for business and this enthralling preoccupation with a dim and imaginary past. Christopher, on the other hand, sought refuge in the glitter of life. He was a true Quixote; he was one of the few beings to whom the term can be applied accurately. Into the loud vulgarity of rich society he stepped all innocently, in the spirit and indeed with the air and appearance, of a paladin of old; his one abiding fault, grave as it was, was essentially a fault of blindness.

I may as well blurt it out at the beginning, for there is, I fear, no avoiding the painful truth: that Christopher was a shocking snob and his tragedy another moral lesson. It furnishes a sermon which is rarely out of season in class-conscious England, but among the causes why I have hesitated before delivering the homily is my consciousness of what great talents have gone before me in this particular pulpit. Sir Max Beerbohm and Mr. Desmond MacCarthy have already overwhelmed congregations with this theme, and I only down pulpit-fright by the recognition of a clear distinction in kind between the calamities of Maltby, Braxton, and Monsieur Bouret, and the fate of Christopher. For whereas my predecessors have dwelt on the woe and ruin attending frustrated snobbism, Christopher illustrates a cruder and older moral: the chastisement which Mammon inflicts on his favourites, the hell to which men can be led by way of the great plush paradises of this world. The story which follows is not new, but neglect may have made it unfamiliar.

At the age of twenty Christopher appears before the world. There is a crayon sketch of him, by Sir Francis Grant as usual, made when he was an undergraduate at Cambridge University around 1850. Very tall, very slender, noble in countenance, the melancholy of the eyes is as yet empty and the classical features lacking in strength. A pale, charming face, slightly epicene in its unusual beauty.

When his second son came of age, old Tatton provided him with comfortable circumstances. He was given a pleasant Jacobean manor-house not far from Beverley, in Yorkshire, which, for the sake of economy, he was commanded to share with a maternal uncle, Sir Henry Foulis. It was the hope of old Tatton that at this house, Brantingham Thorpe, Christopher would become another hero of the hunting field in the country of Holderness, Sir Henry Foulis being his artful though not subtle choice of the furtherance of the plan. This baronet was another, though less volcanic, survival of the former century. His portrait shows him in early middle age, before our period, with ginger curls clustering about his forehead, his hearty countryman's features twisted into an expression of Roman majesty, his immense muscular hands clutching a book and doing what they can to look languid and refined. Tatton felt that such a guardian, knowing nothing of the vanities of London life, would soon wean Christopher from the glitter of his mother's drawing-room (in which he had already achieved some youthful success) and confirm him in the virile ambitions of the chase. But the flexibility of Christopher's nature probably made his father overestimate its weakness. Years of withstanding the Tattonian oppression had taught Christopher much, and he found Sir Henry Foulis easy game. He loaded him with the tedious side of life at Brantingham Thorpe, and thus gave himself more leisure for his major task: the conquest of London.

During the 'fifties his progress in conquest was gradual. There were reasons for this; Tatton's disapproval was to be avoided, and the obligarchy of fashion was in a mood of fierce exclusion. At that time the "rule of the Dandies," as club historians have termed it, was rapidly declining but was by no means ended. They were fighting their last rearguard action. We think of the dandies to-day with sentimental affection, as being, one and all, men of the stamp of d'Orsay or Bulwer Lytton, but contemporary records tell a very different story. They are described as sitting grouped in the clubs, in the theatres, wherever fashion congregated, sunk in dull silence, broken only by loud insults hurled at any one whose chance appearance or manner happened to displease them. They had taken the art of offensive snobbism to a pitch hardly attempted before. Their spiritual descendants are easily recognised to-day, but in those days such people possessed, or had recently possessed, a very important degree of power. They had ruled the clubs, and from the clubs they had influenced not only the great families but in large measure the House of Commons, for even after the Reform Bill there existed an intimate connection between such places as Boodles, Whites, Brooks, and Parliament, which has since almost wholly disappeared. The clubs were in many ways the equivalents of the modern "Party Machines," and indeed it is far from impossible or even improbable that in their extreme old age the bright efficient party machines of to-day may yield some such high irrationality as "the rule of the Dandies."

The 'fifties were an age of final transition. The dandies were old or ageing men, slowly and with bitter tenacity giving way before the new titans of fashion, the "heavy swells" as they were called by the populace. But these were different from their predecessors in a most important respect: they had no wish to "rule." In large part the dandies had been an extreme, a fantastical assertion of an aristocratic will to yield nothing to rising powers, and one can imagine how that will had been weakened, by alarm at the narrow escape of the 'thirties and 'forties, and by the prospect, vivid to men of the time, that civilisation in Macaulay's words, might have been destroyed by the barbarism it had engendered. It had been weakened, too, perhaps, by a sly gratitude at having got off so cheaply. The "heavy swells," no matter how portentous their bearing, entertained slighter ambitions. Pleasure, not power, was their aim. In the slow, semiconscious way of human societies men were forming themselves into an order more adaptable for defence against the contemporary threat, and, surprising effect, the clubs and the world of fashion were becoming less of an industry and more of a complicated game. Unlike the dandies, the "swells" were more purely frivolous.

Gently, imperceptibly, Christopher joined their number.

The family circle in London provided a useful base for his patient campaign. The house had acquired high fashionability as the scene of receptions which were attended by the Duke of Wellington. Christopher learned there the complex art of paying desired attentions to the great, to the rising great, and the setting great. He learned other important lessons too. Once or twice it occurred that in the midst of his mother's entertainments there would burst in the old Yahoo from Yorkshire in his boots and spurs (for like his contemporary, Colonel Sibthorpe of Lincoln, he had an aversion to railways, and even to coaches), and on these rare occasions Christopher observed the deftness with which his mother stowed the old man away out of sight. Old Tatton, recognising his limitations, suffered himself to be controlled thus in London, but it is interesting to note that the brief glimpses he obtained of his younger son in the hated smart world even impressed that gross old man. "Aye," he confided to a fellow-centaur in Yorkshire, "ee's a clever lud is Chris. Ee knoa's oo t'hond leadies in curriage. Ee's a regular Broomel is Chris."

This phase in Christopher's career of conquest lasted for a little more than ten years. In the early 'sixties his parents died—his mother in 1861, his father, to the unaffected relief of the family, in 1863. By this time Christopher had made himself into a well-known man of fashion.

To a casual observer it might have seemed for a moment that he now resolved to quit Vanity Fair in order to direct his footsteps along the stony path of public toil, for in 1865, when he was thirty-four years of age, he entered the House of Commons as the member for

Beverley. But a careful observer, such as the author of *Punch's* "Essence of Parliament," might have perceived that the deliberations of the State were never likely to excite his serious concern. Christopher is described in the act of taking his seat, standing with drooping eyelids and head slightly tilted to the side, as the ancient ceremonies were enacted at the bar. He took the oath. As he was leaving, he noticed the Speaker leaning towards him. He peered at him in curiosity, noticed his outstretched hand, and after touching the tips of his fingers strolled out into the lobby. That, with a wealth of ponderous sarcasm, is the description of *Punch*. Though the implied arrogance is probably a libel, it gives a vivid if distorted picture of Christopher's high antique grace. He was a popular and even conscientious member, but he displayed no vestige, or, to be accurate, only one vestige, of serious interest. He sat in the House of Commons from 1865 to 1892, and in that long interval he made in all six speeches and asked three questions. Disraeli's career was a gradual abandonment of dandyism. Christopher was more faithful to his first avocation.

We may now fairly consider Christopher as he approaches the eminence to which he aspired, in the first radiance of his magnificence.

We look back from the slaughter-house of to-day to that calm noon of high Victorianism with nostalgia and envy. Its solid furniture, its teeming wealth, "its objects," as a later recorder, Henry James, noted them, "massive and lumpish in silver and gold, in the forms to which precious stones contribute, or in leather, steel, brass, applied to a hundred different uses or abuses," together with the triumphant parade of domestic virtue, seem to us to assemble in a stupendous panorama of contentment; coarse, unimaginative, unintelligent, perhaps, but contentment authentic and unexampled none the less. The error has been corrected many times. It has been pointed out that the sense of precariousness which haunted the first half of the century persisted, that the great cult of "respectability" was not a mode of self-expression, but an anodyne adopted by people who pictured disaster as imminent. Our forebears, we are assured, were as inwardly tormented as ourselves. Well, that may be so, but I have a suspicion that in their excitement at having uncovered the hidden impulses of that age, modern critics underestimate the importance of the obvious surface. Any doubts which I have experienced that the later nineteenth century was in truth an age of grave and sincere tranquillity are dispelled by the image of Christopher, that age's greatest fop and dandy.

Where the fops of other ages took the butterfly as their model, he found inspiration in heavier matter. Dignity, majesty, and beautiful gloom, rather than brilliant skimming coloured parabolas, provide the keynote of his style. There is a remarkable half-length portrait of him by Pellegrini made about this time. He has changed much in appearance since his first upward footsteps in the 'fifties. The epicene beauty of youth has given way to a formidable grandeur of mien. The melancholy eyes are set at a downward angle from the fine thin nose, the whole face gives an impression of angularity and length, terminating in a drooping moustache and a long, golden beard. The lofty forehead is surmounted by gloriously well-brushed hair. From his abnormal height he has developed a stoop, not of one loaded with burdens, but such as would not have ill-befitted a Roman Emperor—indeed, his visage bears a certain resemblance to the bust of Antoninus Pius. It is difficult to reconcile this massive appearance, this face which might have done service for the wisest of mankind, with the uncontrollable frivolity which was in fact the principle of his nature, and which led him to founder in coarse and frightful tragedy.

There is a second picture by Pellegrini made some five years later. The grandeur, the stoop, the noble condescension are all there wholly unchanged, but the artist has given redoubled attention to the clothes. One sees what an impressive thing the old white top-hat could be, and how the later dreary version of the frock-coat could assume the proportions of a work of art, following the figure in exquisite rhythm and disciplined variation; but the point which is instantly apprehended as the difference between the dandy and the well-dressed man is that the former literally shines. His tie, his boots, his tall white hat send out gleam upon gleam. He is a work of art. One glance at this fine caricature makes it easy for me to believe what I have been told by elderly people who knew him: that his carriage and grace made those about him seem common.

The second caricature bears a legend, at first sight out of harmony with the figure it portrays: "The Gull's Friend." This nickname derived from his Parliamentary career. Contemporary members may smile at his six speeches and three questions, but he achieved what few of them do to-day. In 1869 he introduced a private members' bill for the preservation of sea-birds, and it passed into law. From this he obtained the nickname. It clung to him for life. The double meaning was intended.

But the House of Commons plays no part in the story. The tragedy was not acted on that humdrum workaday stage. The attention should be diverted from the Palace of Westminster to the northerly side of St. James's Park. That is where Christopher wrought his wonders. The splendours and follies depicted by Thackeray were increasing, both in momentum and in the corpulence of vulgarity; the hideous glories of flunkeydom were setting amid violent glows of ostentation; and to add design to the whirligig of fashion, the insane proceedings of society had found a president in the young lately wed Prince. There he stood, the Lord of London, with his inscrutable German eyes, his Tudor face, his gross pleasures, and more and more frequently there appeared by his side the huge, beautiful mournful form of Christopher.

While the explanation of all deep friendships lies ultimately in the inexplorable depths of the human heart, there are several guesses which, taken together, seem to solve much of the riddle of this once famous attachment, an attachment which, though it destroyed Christopher utterly, yet also opened for him such depths of childish delight. Christopher was ten years older than the Prince, they had certain important psychological conditions in common: both had felt in childhood an unusual weight of parental authority, and from the resulting complex had found in the romance of fashion an escape and anodyne. To the younger man Christopher appeared in the deliciously combined rôles of a sage worldly counsellor and of an irresistible minister of pleasure. To Christopher —well, though everyone who knew him testifies to the sweetness and gentleness of his character, there is no avoiding the fact, as I have already warned my readers, that he had an overriding weakness for which I regret that there is no inoffensive word in existence. He was an unredeemed snob; a snob, I fear, even by the standards of those intolerably snobbish days.

The Prince, of course, was not wholly a creature of romance. He found Christopher extraordinarily useful. To begin with, there was the Prince's taste for horse-racing, in the indulgence of which he liked to be entertained not only with the maximum of comfort and splendour but in strict accordance with his idiosyncrasies: he was fastidious in his vulgarity. For the great Doncaster meeting in September, the meeting for the last classic of the season, the St. Leger Stakes, he found exactly what he wanted at Brantingham Thorpe. The distance to Doncaster by rail was convenient, and Christopher had carriages in attendance at either end. The entertainment was lavish throughout, the guests were perfectly suggested, and disposed about the table with admirable tact, imagination, and correctitude; nor was there any whim of the Prince which was not immediately and abundantly translated into fact. Did he wish to gamble, there were the very newest and best counters, cards, tables, and whatnots; did he wish to dance, there was the best of orchestras; and did he wish for some innocent royal horse-play, that was also to hand, as will appear more clearly later. There is in existence a photograph taken on the first of these occasions. The Prince and his beautiful Princess stand in the centre 'of the picture. Nestling close to the Princess is a foreign queen, a royal duke is artistically placed in the left middle distance. On the other side, enormous, droops the slender figure of Christopher, his beard the least bit stirred by a passing breeze. In the background is what appears to be a midget luggage-van, with the Prince's emblems on it. Scrutiny with a magnifying glass discovers this to be the photographer's technical transport. The year is 1869, and the day must have been one of the happiest in Christopher's life, happy with delicious thrills, doubts, and reliefs, every harassing moment bright with the promise of fame.

The house, fashionable since ten years, was hereafter hallowed, and there begins a succession of sumptuous entertainments, now for hunting, now for shooting, now once again for the St. Leger, while the scene is crowded to capacity with great names. Among the few Christopherean relics which have survived are tomes filled with photographs of these assemblies and others in the great houses of England where, it is testified, so great was Christopher's triumphant fashionability, that the absence of his signature in the visitor's book was to be accounted as some dowdiness. The great melancholy man looms in the background, the head always at the slight characteristic tilt, the clothes always a little more beautiful than the imagination would evoke, the supreme dandy, and yet always with a curious uneasy look in the eyes, suggesting perhaps that the pleasures of snobbism depend in part on a continuance of that stimulating nervousness which accompanies first footsteps in the brilliant mocking world. It is a fine assortment of smartness and history.

The tomes contain a considerable collection of snob masterpieces.

As one appraises them, one is left with the impression that few indeed are the great house parties which can vie in choice majesty with those held at Brantingham Thorpe. The house itself, from being a pleasant, modest Jacobean manor, was enlarged to the dimensions of a stately seat in the revived Jacobean style, but the painful vulgarities attending this familiar experiment were avoided; the furniture, for example, was not Jacobean or revived Jacobean, but eighteenth century, and in the finest taste. In spite of the enlargements the house was never immense, the parties were small by the large standards of the time; Christopher was refined in an age of heavy bigness. The choice of the guests displays the exquisite sense of fashionable values for which he was so justly admired. There is always a solid groundwork of historic peerages in which a few famously "fast men" are cunningly included. Taking the latter as a fresh starting-point, a few of the new vulgarians, those loud, extremely rich men for whom the Prince had an abiding taste, are harmoniously worked into the structure. Eminent politicians of the worldly kind and a famous journalist, or other piece of decoration, are firmly built in, while, in almost every case, the pyramidal point is supplied by the rapidly fattening figure of the Prince himself. He is the inspiration though not the rule. Sometimes a party is assembled about other royalty: that uniquely uninteresting man, the Duke of Cambridge; a massive German couple, the Duke and Duchess of Saxe-Weimar; the Crown Prince of Hanover; and I have wondered sometimes whether, as a man always ready to oblige in the feasting of kings, Christopher was not used in an unscrupulous way by Government officials, for amid these trophies of great English and German princes there survives an unexplained photograph of a negro potentate.

But other beings in whom flowed the royal blood were

as bye-day sport compared to the Prince. He it was and he alone who had conferred hallows on Holderness, and the achievement was the work of Christopher. In the transmogrification of Brantingham Thorpe into a temple of kingliness my uncle had successfully reached the limits of his ambition—he had done what he set out to do. However . . . perhaps he overlooked the fact, perhaps he rashly gambled against it, that the great guest was as tyrannical as he was affable, that the lord of fashion, for all his great girth, was a hurtling Will o' the Wisp. Perhaps as the beautiful bearded man looked down his monstrously laden table, where the coiffures, tiaras, and necklaces alternated with the white cravats, precious studs, whiskers and beards, a thrill of premonition some-times transfixed his sensitive mind as his eye lighted on the robust groomed face of Lord Hardwicke. That unfortunate earl (who deserves a place in history as the inventor of the polished silk hat) had followed a similar career to Christopher's some ten years before, in the course of which he accompanied the Prince on his tour of India. He also became involved in the same fatal game, first of competitive and then of commanded entertain-ment, but (Christopher may have reflected with some comfort) with the disadvantage of having to vie with Oriental despots in splendour and to use elephants among the pieces on the board. The dreadful fact remained that, as a result, Lord Hardwicke lost a large part of his fortune. He was fated to lose the home of his ancestors also. Christopher was not unintelligent. He must have seen that he was playing a dangerous game.

Has someone been forgotten? What had become of Uncle Foulis? He was all right. He was upstairs enjoying a capital dinner in his room. He was happy and invisible. In the first days of the magnificence the good man had seen plain that he was not made for this kind of thing. Christopher agreed. He had foreseen this. It has been noted that he absorbed a useful lesson from the stowing of the elder Tatton in the early 'fifties, and without the suspicion of an unkind word or a hint at anything but the worthy baronet's convenience, he coaxed him into solitary recreation at such times. Uncle Foulis lived happily to the end of his days.

Christopher's troubles began in earnest early on in the 'seventies. He made the error of taking a handsome house in Hill Street, quite large enough for the purposes of royal entertainment. The Prince took careful note. Mightily satisfied with his experiences at Brantingham Thorpe, always anxious, the mischievous said, to save a little money, always glad of an agreeably appointed drawing-room in which gambling "within the reasonable and harmless limits which he always insisted upon" might go forward, the Prince saw no reason why he should not honour his friend freely in London. And, having taken this decision, he not only stuck to it for many years, but was amazed at its success. The Prince often said that there was no host in London or the country who could compare with "dear old Christopher." He was impressed not only by the polish and sobriety of these occasions, their cheer and their respectfulness, their dash and their smoothness, but by the almost incredible speed with which ambitious dinners could be put together without any stray sign in the result of hurried composition. All manner of strange, wild millionaires were wandering round London then, and the Prince, perhaps recognising natural soul-mates, yearned to make these men his friends. All sorts of precedents and inhibitions stood in the way, but Christopher could produce the unique, the flawless occasion for the encounter. He knew how to mix the traditional guardians and companions of the throne with the new raucous offspring of Mammon, and to mix them to such a nicety that not only was discord dispelled but a most pleasing novel harmony brought to charm. The Prince found Christopher invaluable, and in the myopic way of the fortunate he began to overplay his great new toy. Commands would arrive from his house giving Christopher only a week's notice. Commands having been met, the next ones to arrive gave a couple of days. Before very long the Prince would send round a note to Hill Street in the morning requesting a dinner the same evening. And these commands were met too. Christopher's large income began to show signs of contracting rapidly.

This, worry enough, was by no means all. By no means! The note of horror has been wanting hitherto. Sometime in those gorgeous days in the 'seventies this note was introduced by a very dreadful episode. Shortly before, the Prince, moved with impatience at the excessive conservatism of Whites, had founded the Marlborough Club, of which Christopher was a foundation member. It was at the Marlborough that the dreadful episode occurred. A supper was in progress after a late sitting of the House of Commons. Christopher was sitting next to the Prince, when the latter, moved by heaven knows what joyous whim, emptied a glass of brandy over his friend's head.

It may be recalled that Boswell tells of a similar royal assault on General Oglethorpe.

"The General told us that when he was a very young man . . . he was sitting in a company with a Prince of Wirtemberg. The Prince took up a glass of wine, and by a fillip, made some of it fly in Oglethorpe's face. Here was a nice dilemma. To have challenged him instantly might have fixed a quarrelsome character on the young soldier; to have taken no notice of it, might have been considered as cowardice. Ogelthorpe, therefore, keeping his eye upon the Prince, and smiling all the time, said: 'Mon Prince, that's a good joke: but we do it much better in England;' and threw a whole glass of wine in the Prince's face."

If only Christopher had followed that excellent man's example! Perhaps he would not have carried the whole company with him as Oglethorpe did; it might have meant the end of the great attachment; but how much more desirable, even that privation, than what in fact followed.

When the brandy landed on his hair and trickled down his face to the golden beard, Christopher showed a rare thing: an excess of presence of mind. Not a muscle moved. Then, after a pause, he inclined to the Prince and said without any discernible trace of annoyance or amusement: "As Your Royal Highness pleases." The effect of this is recorded as being quite indescribably funny. The whole room burst into violent paroxysms of laughter, and no one laughed more heartily, and certainly not more loudly, than the Prince. Laughter begat laughter, the jest was prolonged till the very act of mirth was unbearable. Christopher dripped. Without a smile on his face he made no effort to mop up the tiny rivulets of spirit. The brandy had been poured by a royal hand. It was sacred. I would give much to know just how much conscious humour there was in Christopher's performance. I believe there was none.

The Prince flattered himself that he had made a discovery. Always an enthusiast for comedy, he had lighted on the greatest comic act of his time: to heap farce and buffoonery upon the Antonine figure of his friend and enjoy the contrast between clowning and persistent dignity, here was an absolutely infallible formula. One of the Prince's weaknesses has already been remarked in this story—namely, that with the secret of eternal youth he retained the child's pure enthusiasm which no amount of repetition can dim, and having enjoyed the great game of sousing Christopher once, he wanted to have it, in the touching way of infancy, "again." Well, royalty can command, and he had it again, he had it unnumbered times, he had it to the very end.

The Marlborough was the usual scene, but Brantingham Thorpe also was allowed to become a royal playground, as were a few of the brighter great houses. The

Prince's simple taste liked enlargement. In place of the glass a full bottle was substituted, and another royal discovery was that even funnier effects could be conjured by pouring the precious liquid not on to his hair, but down his friend's neck. Amid screams of sycophantic laughter the Prince invented an entirely new diversion. Christopher was hurled underneath the billiard-table while the Prince and his faithful courtiers prevented his escape by spearing at him with billiard-cues. And there were further elaborations of the sousing theme. Watering cans were introduced into Christopher's bedroom and his couch sprinkled by the royal hand. New parlour games were evolved from the Prince's simple but inventive mind: while smoking a cigar he would invite Christopher to gaze into his eyes in order to see the smoke coming out of them, and while Christopher was thus obediently engaged, the Prince would thrust the burning end on to his friend's unguarded hand. And the basis of the joke never weakened. To pour brandy down the neck of some roaring drunken sot of a courtier was one thing; but Christopher remained the statuesque figure he had been on the great night of the brandy glass. He never failed his audience. Never. His hat would be knocked off, the cigar would be applied, the soda-water pumped over his head, and he would incline, and murmur: "As Your Royal Highness pleases."

On one occasion the Prince attended a fancy-dress ball. Christopher accompanied him, dressed in complete steel. As they approached the house, the Prince declared that to avoid making a public appearance in his costume he had arranged for the party to be let in by the back door. It was a plot and it succeeded. As the party entered, Christopher found himself last, and, at the moment when he was about to walk in, the door was slammed and locked. He knocked. He knocked many times. He knocked in vain. As the minutes went by, the unusual spectacle began to attract a crowd of curious people. The house into which he so passionately wished to go was one of those immense built-round family palazzos whose back door was in a part of London not distant from, perhaps, but not sharing life with, the region in which the front door was situated, so much so, in fact, that the inhabitants of the back-door area had not become involved in the excitement in front. They had not heard about it. What they saw was a knight fully armed standing in a street. Christopher saw that there was nothing for it: he must walk down the street, turn left up the next street, second right, and then left down to the main street, and so left again to the front door. Normally five minutes, six in armour. It is said that, when he arrived, the vociferous crowd which he brought with him was large enough to add a good third to the numbers already assembled about the front door. Six minutes in armour can be a very long time.

Among the Prince's many practical jokes, this episode of the armour appears to be the only one in which his unflagging cruelty is redeemed by wit. He had much to put up with in Paradise, had the Gull's Friend.

Is it possible that he enjoyed these practical jokes—these hideous outbursts of high spirits among men far past their youth? The answer is that he detested every moment of them. He was not one of those unhappy beings who derive pleasurable excitement from humiliation and pain. He was a normal man afflicted with one excessive abnormality: that complex of ill-balanced predilections which we may classify as snobbism. It must not be forgotten that his snobbism was not the ordinary vulgar kind allied to the enjoyment of any or every kind of ostentation: it was deeply romantic. The Prince was an object of unstinted veneration; through a mist of ancient associations of chivalry the Prince to him was Charlemagne and he one of the paladins surrounding him—yes, he was as blind as all that, and of course—this is where the story is ugliest—it was precisely this blindness which informed the Prince's pranks with such inexhaustible comedy.

It must not be supposed, however, that Christopher sunk into a state of total degradation. He was not quite unmanned by his weakness. He did not suffer his martyrdom without protest, nor without protest of an effective sort. He had a certain wit, not the kind which survives in collections of aphorisms, but, rather, the short-range and sometimes highly formidable kind which depends on allusion and innuendo. The Prince would sometimes find Hanoverian broadsides met by a thrust which went right home and left him momentarily " out ", not so much as a shadow of disrespect having passed. On one occasion Christopher used a more direct method. Following some unusually ferocious outburst, the Prince shouted at him in cacophonous good-fellow-ship: "What d'ye take yerself for, Christopher, hey!" Christopher fixed upon him a stern look. "For," he replied, "Your Royal Highness's obedient, loyal and most tried servant." It is said that the unexpected and awful solemnity of his tone reduced the Prince to silence for the moment, and to civilised behaviour for some weeks.

But there could be no turning back. Having committed his capital error, this gentle loyal man found himself in Macbeth's predicament: stepped in so far, that should he wade no more, returning were as tedious. Mature chronic snobbism, as Dr. Ponde would be the first to admit, allows of no remedy, and it is at this point in the sermon that the preacher's voice must rise to its highest monitory bellow echoing in the dim heights of the upper arches and the hollow lantern. For the fearful truth is that whereas grosser evils can be wiped off a human record, snobbism never can be on account of a terrible peculiarity. It is not the unforgivable sin—far from it—but it *is* the unrepentable sin. The disillusioned snob may often cry out in bitterness, "All is vanity," and again, "Put not thy trust in princes," but he can never keep wholly away from the objects of his baseless, even his consciously baseless, adoration. No love and no drug exerts a more blasting spell. But to return to the story.

The 'eighties dawned and the routine went on; the photographers turned up to perpetuate a little the hunting, the shooting, the St. Leger Stakes entertainments; their long record remains in the tomes. His family, his agent, his bankers united in supplication that he would abandon his ruinous career of pleasure. He was fifty, he would gladly have agreed to their wishes, if—if he might entertain the Prince for the St. Leger, and perhaps one shooting-party, and perhaps one or possibly two tremendous dinner-parties in London, no more. The thing would be kept within modest limits. Agreement was reached, but in vain. There was a magic in the gay, gruff royal voice outside the bounds of economic calculation; there were joys unknown to bankers in the act of inclining to a request for the tenth dinner in the season and murmuring the words: "As Your Royal Highness pleases." Everything went on, including most of the horse-play, just as it had done in the 'seventies. But the moments of stark sobriety were more frequent. The photographs turn to a sadder key.

Christopher's beard is beginning to turn grey. He is no longer the heaviest of the heavy swells. Beside his younger guests, dashing young men with short curly hair and neat though large moustaches, he begins to strike a note of survival. His dress, in the manner of ageing men, becomes fixed in a rigid style. For the St. Leger, which in those days shared the honour of compulsory formal dress with all the major race meetings, Christopher cannot only compete with but can absolutely outshine the younger men in smartness. His silk hat, lapels, boots, tie, shine as only a great dandy's can shine. But on less imposing occasions he begins to appear slightly quaint. The young men wear the newest varieties of bowler hat, while Christopher sticks throughout to that high-domed compromise between the bowler and top hats whose life Mr. Churchill has prolonged to

our own time. Later they all wear the Homburg hat.
But not Christopher; he sticks in his grey hairs to
the hat which was an innovation in his youth. The
clothes suggest the same predicament as the hat: they
are faintly "sixtyish"; more impressive, certainly,
than the others, not quite so fashionable. But the major
difference between this Christopher of the 'eighties and
the great golden figure of the 'seventies appears in
the deepening gloom of the face. The affected melancholy gives way to a sincere, helpless regret. Doom is
near.

The ever-fresh appetite of the Prince and the weakness
of his friend kept the mechanism in operation until early
in the nineties. Then came the crash. It came inevitably.
It happened simply thus: Christopher was approaching
old age, the possibility of marriage with an heiress had
passed, his income was less than half its original figure,
his debts were enormous. So the creditors closed in.
They found insolvency, they proposed bankruptcy.
"What a thoroughly bad business!" exclaimed the
Prince when he heard of it.

The stricken paladin was far too noble-mannered to
appeal for aid, but surely he had the right to hope that
his Charlemagne would hear the winding of a horn from
the deep forest of despair; that he would remember the
long, patient fidelity, the reckless generosity, the luxury
and the loyalty that had never been withheld. Well, if
he hoped, he hoped in vain. The Prince had his own
very considerable troubles. The years succeeding that
dreadful business at Tranby Croft were not easy ones in
which to tap the royal bounty, especially on behalf of
one of the guests at that notorious affair. "What a
thoroughly bad business!" he cried, and (so he supposed)
was obliged to let it go at that. But here he made a
curious miscalculation. The winding of the horn was
indeed heard and help did come, but from an unexpected
quarter.

Christopher had a sister-in-law with whom he had

never been on very intimate terms. She appears only once in the accumulation of the Brantingham photographs. She was a woman of Napoleonic energy, with a passion for life as deep as Christopher's, but, unlike his, a hearty and unrestrained passion. Her eccentric and violent temperament had proved a considerable anxiety to her friends, and her scorn of all conventions kept the excessively conventional Christopher in a state of steady disapproving alarm. On her side she had not given any sign of being very fond of her brother-in-law. She regarded him as a fool and said so frequently. She had a gift for satire and mimicry which she used without much charity. She was the last person from whom the poor man would have expected aid, but her very being was made up of contradictions: there was a heavenly generosity in her spirit which, like so much about her, was intense and even terrible. In a great rage she came down to London bent on rescue.

There was no doubt in her mind from what source rescue was to be drawn. It was the Prince's fault, she said simply, so the Prince must pay. The Prince did not know her very well, but, accurately informed as always, he knew not only of her disorders but of her unforgivable remarks about himself and some of his friends. However, she was not easy to withstand. No barriers solid enough had yet been contrived to keep this impossible woman from where she happened to want to go. She could be irresistibly femine or unbearably domineering, not only by turns, but, what was so disconcerting, simultaneously. Her smile and engaging lisp were sometimes accompanied by eyes blazing forth in fire; hammering logic mingled with screaming farce; thunder with sunshine. What happened at her interview with the Prince is not known. The stories about it are too contradictory or too melodramatic to command belief, while the two people who knew the truth left no record. What is known is that, shortly after the crash, she went in high fury and by appointment to the Prince's great house in

London, was closeted with him for a short time and then left. The main part of Christopher's debts was paid.

He was saved from the awful disgrace of bankruptcy, but he was left, for all that, wounded and horseless indeed. Most of his capital had to go; and not only the house in Hill Street, but the hallowed fane at Brantingham Thorpe left his possession for ever. Not much remained. The great dandy was now a poor man, not only by the elevated standards of those days, but by our own.

People sneered that the great attachment was only another case of cupboard love; wait and watch it dissolve, they sniggered. In this they were wrong. Evil nature was not in the Prince. The friendship went on, in much the same uproarious manner as before, not mercifully in a turmoil of practical jokes, but with roars of coarse rallying, back-slapping and broadsides. And the old broken courtier still had the spirit to send back keen respectful arrows into the bowels of the attacking craft. Nevertheless nothing could hide the grim fact of the fall; the 'nineties were a long process of deepening twilight. The great host was now an eternal guest. Wearily, mournfully, from habit as much as anything else, the melancholy man journeyed from house to house, from comital to ducal pile, from dukeries to royalty, and back again, to and fro. He had left the House of Commons in 1892, and he now had very little with which to occupy his mind. He who had spent so recklessiy now had to count every coin; his visits to the great houses began to become noticeably protracted. Nor was he now pre-eminent in the glory of dress and dandyism. As he declined, a new sun was rising, outshining him as he had outshone thirty years before. In the later photographs the first figure to seize the attention is that of Lord Chesterfield—immaculate, beautiful, whether in formal, ordinary, or sporting dress. He stands forth from pampered crowds magnificent and erect, while Christo-

pher's once impressive studied stoop is the bent attitude
of an old and tired man. It was a fall indeed.

It would be better if the story ended here, but Christopher had a little farther to go, nor were his woes quite
terminated. Among the miseries which thickened about
his last years ill health took a place. He was a delicate
man, years of sumptuous eating had put a strain on his
innards the effects of which were becoming serious. An
important part of his small income was devoted to a
yearly cure at Homburg; and it was during one of these
necessary periods of retirement that he met his end under
extraordinary and yet apallingly appropriate circumstances. One day in the summer of 1898, while Christopher was undergoing the most drastic cure yet attempted
upon him, an event occurred on the royal yacht which
was destined to have wider consequences than at first
appeared. The Prince slipped up on board, and in falling
sprained his ankle very severely. He was carried to his
cabin, his medical advisers assured him that the wrench
had very nearly caused dislocation, and insisted that he
should not rise from his couch for several days. To the
Prince the pleasures of illness were a closed book, as were
most books when they lay in his plump hands. He was
quite defenceless against the pains of boredom. Where
was Christopher? What! At Homburg! Good gracious,
send him a telegram immediately! See that arrangements
are made for him to be met at Ostend! See that he's here
by to-morrow! See that a cabin is got ready for him!

A reply came from Homburg. Christopher presented
his duty; he asked leave to sympathise with His Royal
Highness in his mishap, which he was deeply relieved to
learn was not as grave as might have been anticipated
at first. He begged to be allowed to express a hope for His
Royal Highness's swift recovery. With submission he
must with great regret ask His Royal Highness to excuse
him from accepting the very gracious invitation to attend
His Royal Highness on board. He had consulted his
medical man, who had assured him that any break in the

cure he was undergoing might have grave and incalculable consequences. His Royal Highness would appreciate the very sincere regret and disappointment which he felt at being obliged to send such a reply.

The Prince was roused to anger. Never once in the many years he had known him had Christopher failed him. He had asked him to do preposterously difficult things and he had done them, now he asked him to do an easy thing and he refused. In a moment of impatience he dictated a second telegram. . . .

In Brussels Christopher had a few hours between trains. He spent part of them sitting in the sun in those pleasant gardens which lie like a miniature Tuileries in front of the palace. There he met, by chance, a stout young man, a guest of former days, by name Lord Vaux of Harrowden. To him he confided that he felt the end of his life drawing on quickly, and he seemed disturbed as to how he could support the strain of his impending visit. "I have tried to explain," he said. Valiantly he went on. He stayed on board for a few days. He had no vitality. He looked very old and very ill. The Prince noted the change, and did not press him to stay on when he asked permission to go home. He went back to England and died.

When he heard the news the Prince was seized with remorse. He realised what he had done. For the first time, perhaps, he realised how much blame he incurred for the whole ghastly episode, and he was smitten by a gust of grief such as was rare with him. Selfish as he was, there is no doubt that the affection he felt for Christopher was in essence warm and generous.

I should like that to be the end of the story, but Christopher's adventures continued a little farther than death. For his besetting fault Fate was hard on this mild sweet-natured man.

The Prince, moved by a good-hearted wish to make amends, decided to travel to Yorkshire for the funeral at

Brantingham Thorpe, and he was accompanied by an immense concourse of fashionable mourners. It was to be such a funeral as Christopher might have wished for—as sumptuous and as distinguished as any frolic for the St. Leger had been. The ceremony went forward impressively, with never a hitch or flaw. Until the final scene at the grave. The diggers had not calculated the abnormal length of the coffin. The grave was of ordinary size. When the pathetic moment arrived for the coffin to be lowered it remained on the surface. It did not fit the grave. Attempts were made to lower it crookedly, feet foremost, then head foremost. And then someone remembered the brandy glass. One or two suddenly turned away. Then the Prince got out his handkerchief. The officiating ecclesiastic signed to the undertakers to leave the coffin where it was. The ceremony went on, and the reading of the great and inspired words was interrupted by gulps, artificial coughings, and the use of more handkerchiefs than tears. Would it were not so, but The Gull's Friend, even in death, could not escape from the comedy which pursued him like a harpy, which pursued him literally to the grave.

The epilogue is brief. A year or so later a subscription for a memorial to Christopher was raised by his friends, the money being entrusted to the Prince for disposal. "A memorial to dear old Christopher!" he exclaimed. "Well, now, what about a clock over the stables?" It is said, how truly I do not know, that Lord Rosebery recommended that a tablet would be more fitting. At all events the tablet was erected, and still testifies to the friendship of those two very different men.

Two years later, in 1901, the Victorian reign came to an end. Henry James wrote from London to a friend living in Paris, "We all feel motherless to-day. We are to have no more of little mysterious Victoria, but instead fat vulgar dreadful Edward." One wonders whether the old Queen had ever heard of the awful saga of Brantingham Thorpe and Hill Street. Probably it was carefully kept from her, but she had sharp eyes and ears. If she did hear, I feel that she was not amused.

Is there anything to add to the end of Christopher's story? The moral is so plain, the wheel of folly and chastisement comes full circle so perfectly that only a dunce could miss the lesson. And yet . . . I wonder sometimes whether there is not something esoteric in the story, something of great and once obvious importance now invisible in the confusion of decay. To be loved long after death is not the lot of many impoverished old bachelors, but Christopher's name was honoured with that rare and lovely tribute. I am thinking in particular of a strangely moving homage which was paid to his memory. One of his nephews was Admiral Sir William Pakenham, whose name may now be little remembered, though he was well known as a distinguished and fearless naval commander at the time of the first World War. He was a man of severe and beautiful character. In his youth he knew Christopher well. Every year, on the anniversary of Christopher's death, he journeyed to Yorkshire to visit his uncle's tomb at Brantingham Thorpe. Not once when he was in England did he neglect this pious act, from 1898 to the year preceding his death in 1935. I cannot believe that such a man would have made such an offering to mere hollow foolishness, and the recollection of it is a salutary check to pompous sententiousness. The past is often as much distorted as clarified by the distance of time. Much has been said of the artistry of memory, but it is too facile an interpreter for the ultimate purposes of History; it preserves garish highlights but neglects the deeper shades.

2

THE INSPIRATION OF A PERSIAN

" If, then, the tree may be known by the fruit, as the fruit by the tree, then, peremptorily I speak it, there is virtue in that Falstaff."   HENRY IV. PART I.

"THE DEATH of Bahram Kirmani will recall to many the amusing personality, who for several years acted as cicerone to Englishmen who had the uncommon good fortune to visit Isfahan. To these the memory of the mosques of Isfahan, the memory of those radiantly tiled interiors which were not open to European visitors until so recently, these jewels of experience, will be for ever associated with the original and delightful old gentleman who first organised privileged visits. No Englishman felt a stranger to Isfahan after he had met Bahram ; he was, in his charming and unconventional way, the perfect informal go-between. While Bahram's profound knowledge of the Sufi mystics of Iran has proved to many of his English friends the starting-off point in one of the greatest adventures of the mind, the study of Persian religious verse, it is equally true that he brought to his own countrymen an infectious understanding of English ideas, and was probably one of the most effective exponents of our ideals and aims anywhere abroad. Part of his education was obtained in England, and in consequence of this he always preserved for this country a feeling of deep devotion. He was a loyal friend in the darkest days, and in his death many Englishmen must feel that we have lost one of those *amis de la maison* whose position is as gracious as it is rare."

That is from an obituary notice which appeared in a learned journal when the news of Bahram's death was received here in 1945. I wrote it myself. I had to write something, so I wrote that. I suppose it was what was wanted, but I knew well what was in his mind when a friend of mine from Persian days wrote me a postcard saying that he had read and enjoyed my memoir, but that he hoped that something else might in time be written about this unusual man, "the unexpurgated edition," as he said with meaning. Yes, indeed. I have never felt comfortable about my obituary of poor Bahram. I dislike the style in which those sort of articles are written, the assumption of reverence, the hollow honours heaped on "the departed," the platitudinous catalogue of virtues; and applied to my friend, this ancient manner of celebrating the awful mystery of death sounded particularly meaningless. No, on such a subject it were wrong to exchange the violent poetry of the facts for the anæmic beauties of convention. Let me try to make amends now.

Persia is an overwhelming and terrible memorial to the transitoriness of earthly things. That immense plateau, once rich and well populated, is now a gaunt waste. Where great cities once flourished in the prosperous barbarity of the ancient empires, small villages, disfigured by a poverty terrible to see, mark an historic site. Directions are sometimes most easily maintained by following mouldered tumuli which were once the strongholds of conquerors. Long ago all reliance on permanent human institutions was abandoned here. Persia is as scattered with wrecks as the ocean bottom, and from a distance it is not easy to tell whether a particular ruin is Macedonian, Medieval, or twentieth century. "Look and despair" is written large and legibly over that fearful, ravaged, and unspeakably beautiful country.

To say that is true. But it is only half the truth.

Nowhere so beautifully as here is the poetry of the oasis manifest. The spring gushes cold and perfect in the middle of the howling desert. That man cannot be conquered by calamity is another message written smaller but as firmly over the face of that stone-strewn land. The Persian garden is not a legend. Any one who has travelled over those hot, seeming endless plains, ringed about with jagged frowning hills, and who has seen one of the blue domes of Persia glistering in the distance, knows on what the abiding greatness of Persia depends. Once, some years ago, on a lonely sun-baked road, miles from any human habitation, I picked up a starving man and carried him in my car to the next town. What fixed this incident firmly in my memory was the fact that throughout the journey this starving man recited lyrical verses by Hafiz.

This proud and beautiful insistence that man is a joyous creature no matter what miseries may oppress him finds its fullest and grandest expression in the city of Isfahan. Its tiled domes rise up in lovely defiance in the midst of a great grim plain. Many other cities can offer marvellous beauty as the reward of a search, but Isfahan belongs to those few where beauty makes the first, the irresistible impression, and this beauty seems to stay at your side, not to forsake you for an instant, no matter how long you stay. Even in dilapidation, as it now is, even when a scene of horrible starvation as when I last saw it, Isfahan never ceases to enchant the senses with its haunting music, "like of a hidden brook, in the leafy month of June."

In 1931 two English visitors arrived in Tehran from the South in the course of what would now be described as a "global flight." They were Mrs. Edwin Montagu and Mr. Rupert Belville. These aviators, of whom one was reputed to have been the only English woman to have visited the front-line trenches in the First Great War, and the other to have mastered the art of bull-fighting among the adventures of his career, brought with them extra-ordinary news. They related that while in Isfahan on their journey northwards from the Gulf, the Consul-General, Mr. Bristow, had been able to arrange for them to enter the mosques of that city. It is not easy to convey to the general reader what were the revolutionary and exciting implications of these tidings. Up to that moment the interiors of the Persian mosques had been forbidden to all except Moslems. In consequence they had been seen by so few Europeans that no reliable record of them existed; not one single photograph had been taken of them; they were known to us as enchanted views through doorways and no more. Criticism of Persian decorative tile-work depended almost exclusively on examination of gateways, domes, and the Madrassy, or sacred college, of Isfahan, a very spectacular but quite inferior example of this art. That the Isfahan mosques were supreme artistic creations could hardly be doubted after a glance at what little of them could be seen by infidel eyes; they had remained till then one of the most delicious and tempting speculations in the whole realm of architecture and decoration. It is no exaggeration to say that the news brought by the two English travellers was as if we heard that the churches of the city of London were to be open to the public for the first time to-morrow.

How had this been achieved? Their story was as follows. Mr. Bristow had a friend in Isfahan called Bahram, an elderly gentleman now in impoverished retirement, who was reliably reported to be a graduate of Balliol College, Oxford. One day, a little before the arrival of the two travellers, Mr. Bristow had asked this man whether, as Consul, he might be permitted to pay a visit to the principal mosques; and Bahram had replied that as he knew the Governor extremely well he thought he might be able to " arrange something along the lines indicated." And thus, unwittingly, Bahram brought about a revolution in Oriental art criticism. It must be admitted that as a religious man, which he claimed to

be, he seems to have gone to work in a somewhat con-
scienceless fashion; for he gained his end, according to
Mr. Bristow, by pointing out to the Govenor that since
the policy of the government was strongly anti-clerical,
one of the most effective means of gaining favour would
be to authorise visits of unbelievers to the hitherto un-
polluted mosques of the great city. The advice was sound.
Reza Shah's policy at that time was not merely anti-
clerical but anti-Islamic: indeed, he was toying with
the idea of abolishing the Koran in Persia and of con-
verting the religion of Zoroaster into a national church.
Bahram's advice fell on fruitful soil. The Govenor saw
his chance. Unobtrusively, for it was a fearful break
with solemn traditions, the mosques were opened to the
unclean. On a historic day, Mr. and Mrs. Bristow were
conducted round those astonishing masterpieces. Suppose
you were the first person allowed to see the Rubens room
in the Louvre!

Mrs. Montagu and Mr. Belville were only a little
more enthusiastic about the marvels which they had seen
in the mosques—they were, as I reckon, among the first
ten Europeans to see them freely—than they were about
the organiser of these experiences. They both insisted
that Bahram was a very considerable masterpiece himself.
Even had he been "no one in particular" he would have
arrested the dullest attention, they said, but a Balliol
graduate in Isfahan—there was the spice of romance!
They said that his conversation, conducted with a gentle
hint of the old-fashioned Swinburnian intonation of
Oxford, had a gaiety which years had not robbed of any
freshness. He radiated a sort of distinguished comedy
about him. Although it was evident that he had fallen
from a considerably higher station in life than he now
occupied, he seemed above the tedious, if pathetic, art of
the hard-luck story. He disdained sympathy. He was
great, they said, in this: that he seemed to mingle the
pleasant carefree laughter of Oxford with the immortal
smile of the fair city to which in advanced age he had

returned. It must be added that a strict moralist might not have looked upon this mirthful afternoon of life with unqualified approval. Mr. Belville confided to me that at the end of their visit to the great buildings Bahram had drawn him aside to suggest less unusual delights of Isfahan which in exchange for a trifling sum of money he could unlock for him in the evening.

This account of Bahram prompted in us who heard it in Tehran a question and a suspicion: Was he in truth a member of the famous Oxford college? After much deliberation, the two travellers, at least, were prepared to give him the benefit of this insistent doubt. Though Mr. Bristow had withheld judgment, even he had conceded that if he was not a Balliol graduate he certainly knew more about Balliol, about Oxford, about England, than any other human being who had not studied at the elder English University. The more the matter was debated, the more opinion in favour of Bahram's claim grew in weight and volume. It was argued thus: agreed that Balliol is a very eminent college, agreed that Oxford has its snobberies, yet, given all that, it is wholly unnatural, wholly non-Oxonian, for a member of one college to pretend to have been at another. The idea is absurd. Very well then. Accepting thus much by way of premises, a strong case followed. The fact that Bahram had to such perfection all the manners of an Oxford man, and none of the manners of the familiar Oxford fraud, made it probable—a point even Mr. Bristow accepted with reservations—that he had lived in Oxford, and how else should a Persian of slender means live there except as a member of the University? If this was allowed, only one feeble obstacle remained: had he perhaps been a non-collegiate member? A strong advocate, History, here came to his aid. History supported colleges. For judging by his age, it seemed that he must have been one of those Persian students sent to Europe by Nasr ud Din Shah in the 'eighties and 'nineties, and experts answered for it that all those who were sent to

Oxford went to colleges. It followed, step by step, almost irrefutably, it seemed, that Bahram was really and truly a Balliol man.

About seven months after the visit of Mrs. Montagu and Mr. Belville I was staying with Mr. Bristow in Isfahan, and naturally I asked my host whether a visit to the mosques could be arranged for me. Nothing easier, he said; and the next morning I also was introduced to Bahram Kirmani in the pleasant cypress planted garden of the Consulate.

His appearance was very striking. We speak of people being globular, but the expression is usually facetious. To Bahram, however, the term could be applied almost with exactness: the ellipse formed by his outline was very nearly circular. He was strikingly short, too, not much more than five foot, and his continual smile, his well-trimmed grey moustache and grey hair, the abandoned flourish of his stick when he walked, made me think of him, later, when I knew more about his character and history, as a kind of spruce pocket Falstaff. The fact that he was well dressed was noticeable, particularly as he was living in an age of highly unsuccessful Persian costume. In those days of Persian chauvinism a legend had been ordered from the Imperial Palace in Tehran that the Persians were and always had been outstandingly "modern": that the dress of a Persian was, and always had been, a coat, trousers, waistcoat, collar and tie, and (extraordinary detail) a ski-ing cap. Turbans and robes, it was added, had never been known in that part of Asia, and the obedience of the Persians gave the legend outward form. Amid a host of tattered, bewildered, faked Europeans Bahram stood forth as the authentic thing. Yes, he certainly looked like a Balliol graduate (in a ski-ing cap), and the fact that he was for ever fingering an amber rosary gave added plausibility to this romantic figure.

We went off together to the mosques, and there followed for me a very great experience. I saw for the first time the immense splendours of Persian decoration, splendours only comparable with the greatest this world has to show. Imagine myself, a tall, very young Englishman, and this little round, partridge-like figure waddling by my side, pointing his clouded cane in different directions as we walked through the huge Piazza or mingled in the crowds and din of the domed bazaars. "Here, my dear fellow," I can hear him, "we are in the Maidan-i-Shah, the Place Royale, so to speak. Lord Lansdowne once told me that he considered Trafalgar Square the most beautiful object in the world. I replied: ' So might I, my dear, if I had never seen our own Piazza in Isfahan so called.' Vanished days! I had the privilege of teaching Miss Marie Corelli how to smoke opium in the North British Hotel in Edinburgh." Imagine our progress halted by such visions of loveliness that I could only gasp and gasp in speechless admiration. On these occasions Bahram was the perfect guide. He subdued his personality. He respected the need for silence in the presence of these miracles of symphonic colour, and after negotiating with the door-keepers of the mosques (an expensive item) he was always careful to get behind me, so that I should have the experience of entering alone.

It was not till towards the end of the day, when, fatigued with the feast of beauty, we were reposing in the gardens of the palace known as "The Countless Columns," that we began the first of a long series of conversations. He told me of his pride in having caused the opening of the mosques to us infidels. He told me he was a Sufi or pantheistic mystic, belonging to the only type of Islam which can converse with certain schools of Christian practice. The two faiths were not so divided from one another as bigots pretended; his life-work was a humble contribution to world-understanding.

Conversation did not remain permanently on this high level, but, on the other hand, it did not leave the high level for long either. It is not easy to describe the way he talked without giving the impression that his mind was disorderly, which it was not. He was a well-knit single entity, not an assembly of opposites; he was a fusion of contradictory elements; and among the elements, among the wild contrasts of his mind, the most prominent landmark was his deep love and longing for England. Conversation had a way of covering immense distances with Bahram, but it returned most frequently to the topic which for him was the most haunting and irresistible in the world, the England of fifty years ago. God! How that man loved England !

It was clear that he must have spent a long time in this country. He knew things about England which can only be known to those who have spent many years inside it. He was very well read in the English literature of the late nineteenth and early twentieth centuries; he had known many famous writers intimately in their unfamous youth. What gave an authentic note of charm to his manner of reminiscence was that he knew and loved England without having become "déraciné," without becoming one of those maniacs who grow tedious about the foreign country of their choice. He was a real Persian. This was often illustrated in comic ways, not so much by lapses in his over-faultless English, though these occurred, as by Persian surprises in the working of his mind. Here is a nice example of what I mean. One day we were having a serious thoughtful talk about the British Constitution when Bahram said:

"And then, what a fine and inspiring figurehead you have over it all in your Royal Family. It is when you live under a tyranny, such as we have here, that you learn to appreciate what it is to be under sovereigns like King George and Queen Mary."

"Certainly."

"What I mean to say is: they are not always massacring the people." (I liked that "always".)

One afternoon I drove him out in my car to the hill on the southern side of Isfahan from which the whole magical city can be seen in a single panorama. Wonderful, indescribably beautiful sight! We sat down, and Bahram told me the story of his life.

He belonged to a family of Kirman which had migrated in the time of his grandfather to Shiraz. There, his father, having met with the favour of the Prince-Govenor of Fars, became one of his secretaries. The Prince noted his son, the young Bahram, and was struck by his extraordinary intelligence, which appeared, among other things, in an abnormal proficiency in foreign languages. To speak many tongues with grace and fluency is not necessarily a mark of intellectual distinction; it is a gift which the laughing gods often bestow upon dullards, but in the case of Bahram his talent was the measure of his mind. Seeking for learning amid the scant materials of Iran, the youth made himself a master of Persian erudition, of the classical poets, of Koranic law and tradition, and of the Turkish language, both in the idiom of Constantinople and of its mother tongue of Turkestan. He learnt English from missionaries and Russian from merchants. He mastered both, and with his avid taste for reading he was, at the age of seventeen, a moderately well-read man in both languages. He knew London as the city of Dickens, and St. Petersburg as the scene of Dostoyevski's agonies.

The Prince-Govenor was moved from Shiraz to Isfahan, and he took this family of Kirmanis with him. The Emperor, Nasr ud Din Shah, was experiencing at that time one of those passing passions for reform which illuminated his long career of autocracy. Persian youths of promise were being shipped off to foreign lands in order to be educated, it being the belief of their cloudy-minded monarch that, given some hundreds of well-educated subjects, railways and riches could be run up in a matter of weeks, if, indeed, they did not quite magically spring up of themselves. Both Great Britain and Russia were anxious to co-operate in this design. The conflict of interests between those two Powers in Asia was never more acute than then, and both were tempted by the prospect of rearing a generation of Persian political influence favourable to their respective causes. On the Persian side, hotly competing families groomed their boys in English or Slavonic studies in the excitement of this unusual opportunity. But for Bahram the question of selection was not a cause of anxiety: his astonishing gifts and the patronage of the Prince made him so plainly eligible that he and his family were concerned rather with a magnificent doubt as to whether the Universities of England or of Russia would provide the more desirable term to his education. He himself put forward the solution: let England be the scene of education, let Russia be the scene of subsequent enrichment. And so it did in fact come about. On a day in the late 'eighties the young Bahram, surrounded by his weeping relations, looked on the domes of Isfahan for the last time for many years.

According to Bahram, he entered Balliol not as a simple undergraduate but as a scholar. All that he knew about Oxford he had learned from the novels of Thackeray. He was but very imperfectly prepared for the reality, for the bright lawns, the ancient stones, the whispering spires, the grandeur and the homeliness, the companionship, learning and wit of Oxford, and these instantly and marvellously conquered his young and generous soul. He told me that this experience, unimagined because unimaginable, provided the most exquisite sensation of his life, and that never subsequently, crammed with incident and excitement though his life was, did his thoughts stray far from the cloisters of Balliol. This abiding affection was all the more remarkable since it was at Balliol that he first met bitterness and disaster, those dark angels which lurk about very young, very propitious lives. His career opened in brilliance, but during his third year he fell into disgrace, into absolute disgrace: he was expelled or "sent down," as the Oxford phrase is.

The story was not unique. When England takes a stranger to her heart she nearly squeezes him to death. The social success of Bahram at Oxford, leading to even greater triumphs in London, was a prodigy which cannot be contemplated without admiration and envy. The handsome young man, with his black ringlets and his insolent moustache, was immediately accepted by the University as one of its natural lords. Oxford has always been unhampered by convention in her choice of despots, a fact which, when the young man discovered it, he exploited to the very utmost. He knew that the secret lay in the combination of physical and intellectual prowess, but above all in the exercise of wit and charm. None of the conditions were beyond his ability. How, then, did he fall? Amid the delicacies of the feast of Reason he devoured poison.

For all the shining surface of his mind, his inner soul was that of an ordinary believer in Islam. Bahram began to enlarge the scope of his ideas as rapidly as the scope of his acquaintance. A distinguished don with whom he had made friends, struck by the sagacity of the young man, introduced him to the works of Charles Darwin and the great evolutionists. This was the fatal event. It must be remembered that Christianity seemed almost to shrivel to extinction under the first cold novelty of the Darwin theory, but Christianity is not a stranger to pliancy and adaptability. Mercifully for the ministers of religion, nothing compromising is said about the course of creation in the New Testament. Islam is in a far more difficult case. Mahomet, unfortunately for his following, set down revelations on the origin of the Universe which are all too embarrassingly precise. Strict Islam and acceptance of evolution are hardly conjoinable. So Bahram lost his faith. It was replaced by a cult of debauchery, intense as the violence of his despair. It was thus in his third year at Oxford, in an anguish of grief, that he was ejected from the place he loved most on this earth, and which never failed him of inspiration throughout his long life.

Bahram, while glorying in his brief sovereignty at Oxford, or while tasting the delights of London society, during this intoxicating experience of the gold and wine of youth, had not forgotten the careful calculation with which he had opened his career. He had made himself acquainted with the Russian Embassy and with Russian merchants and traders in England; he had artfully made for himself a place in Anglo-Russian sections of London society. Some months before his humiliation at Oxford he had obtained for himself a post in one of the great business houses of St. Petersburg. Thither he now journeyed, and, except for holidays spent in England, he made Russia his home.

By the time he reached the age of thirty he was a very wealthy man. He had a house in St. Petersburg, and one of those wild plaster palaces on the shores of the Black Sea which in old and new Russia are the very synonym of luxury. His career in Russia, according to his own account, was brilliant from its inception. There are few great Russian names of that period which are not the names of his companions: Orloff, Stalipin, Tolstoy, and Tchehov were all friends of this remarkable, this dazzling and meteoric man. But he had developed morbid and repulsive features in his character which the wild life of Russia deepened: the debauchery which had sullied his Oxford days did not pass away with the bloom and follies of youth; it grew into a cancer of his soul. Wealth increased his corruption. For months he would vanish from the glittering society of which, he gave me to understand, he was a considerable ornament, and lie dissolved in vice and drunkenness. Among the friends of this darker side of his nature there was one more evil than the others, one in whom perverted piety was horribly mingled with a passion for excitement mad or satanic in its fury: his name was Rasputin. When the

Revolution came, Bahram was in the Crimea. No longer young, he was now a confirmed and perpetual drunkard; he was soon reduced to absolute penury. He entered a state of degraded wretchedness which was the heavy retribution for his career of license. He had injured all his faculties. He became a beggar. He was lost to shame, or even care, for he had only one care which obliterated all others: a gnawing hunger for alcoholic stimulants, for vodka.

The charity of a countryman enabled him to reach Azerbaijan, the former scholar of Balliol became a beggar of Tabriz.

According to his account, the origin of all Bahram's ills lay in his rejection of religion those many years ago at Oxford. Now in the depths of his despair he recovered his faith. In darkest night the soul of Bahram turned once more to noble things. In the horrid gloom of his life in Tabriz he discovered in the Autobiography of Al-Ghazzali and in the lyrics of Jalal Ud Din Rumi a form of orthodox piety where breadth and greatness of aspiration made Bahram's doubts appear in the proportions of hardly relevant details in a comprehensive system of ideas. It was under the influence of the pious Persian scholar who directed his studies that he renounced the use of strong liquor and, all humbly, repentantly, and triumphantly, dedicated his life to the service of God. This pious man flooded his soul with light; he showed him that his misery was a gift from Heaven, that the Divine Mercy had placed him far on the road to renunciation and beatific vision, and after they had read the sublime Jalal Ud Din together, he commanded Bahram to embrace the calling of Dervish. As a Dervish he returned, forgotten, to Isfahan. Thus ended his story.

As the sun set in majesty over Isfahan I listened to this extraordinary recital. There was a dignity, a wit and a pathos in the way he told it which I cannot attempt to reproduce. His descriptions of London in the last years of the nineteenth century, of Oxford, of the luxury and horror of St. Petersburg, of the conduct of Rasputin, of the difficulties which arose between King Edward and Muzzaffar ud Din Shah, of an unfórtunate meeting with Mr. Balfour, were all of them little masterpieces in their way. Not for one moment did my interest diminish; Bahram had none of the insistent egotism of the raconteur, he had an artist's detachment from his work and from himself: his descriptions of himself, indeed, had an innocent and absolutely irresistible comedy about them. As we drove back in the rapidly falling dark I reflected that I had heard one of the most moving accounts of a life possible to imagine. As a document of human adventure it was marred by only one fault: that hardly one word of it was true.

Shortly after this memorable evening Bahram accompanied me on a journey to the tribal countries of the Bahktiarri, west of Isfahan. The old patriarchal life of Persia was still flourishing in those highlands, the Khans still ruled over their territories in the manner of Norman barons, and I journeyed, taking great delight in everything I saw, as though through a Gothic novel. There grew up between Bahram and myself an intimate friendship which the vicissitudes of time never dimmed but increased. I grew to understand his character, or rather, I should say, that having learned to distinguish and enumerate the enormous number of its ingredients, familiarity led me to accept its strongest contradictions without surprise. Not that the enigma. ever ceased to haunt me.

What was the truth about Bahram? Mr. Bristow, who had a tenacious and refined taste for Persian comedy, had brought to this question a great deal of research, mostly in vain. The first part of the story, the quiet adventures of the Kirmani family leading to young Bahram's departure in search of foreign education, could be and was proved correct until the final detail. Did he leave Persia by the Westward or the Northern gate? The first of all the Bahramic problems soon began to raise its head again, for when research reached that point there was found no record at Oxford of Bahram ever having been at Balliol. This, of course, was no solution, for it left the original and major problem unexplained: how was it that he spoke about Oxford and about the great past figures of Oxford without one false or ill-tuned note? Was Bahram, then, one of the greatest actors the world has ever seen? Or had some man responsible for such things forgotten to write his name down in some book at Balliol years ago?

Mr. Bristow knew the latter part of the story. The holy man of Tabriz was a projection from himself, Mr. Bristow, and the missionary doctor of Isfahan, Dr. Schafter. Mr. Bristow had found poor Bahram in the last stages of delirium tremens, and, moved with compassion, he had arranged for him to be cured at the Mission Hospital. The cure was successful. Mr. Bristow knew nothing about the dark night of the soul; he had never, to tell the truth, heard of its existence before, but he could explain its place in Bahram's story. During his long residence in Persia as a Consular officer, Mr. Bristow had made a study of the Persian classics, of which he had become a proficient amateur. He was much attracted to the Massnavi I Ma'navi of Rumi, and when Bahram had recovered his wits he used to help him to read those inspired verses. "The curious thing," Mr. Bristow added, bubbling with laughter, "is that though you cannot believe a word Bahram says, he is not a deceitful or unreliable man. He is perfectly sincere. He is a very faithful friend. He lives in that poetic borderland whose landscape seems as familiar to most Persians as a meadow and hedges are to you and me. *I* don't know whether he was at Balliol or not—he must have got his enormous education *somewhere*—but the point is he *feels* as if he had been to Balliol, and so, as far as he's concerned, he *was* at Balliol. Persians are Christian scientists upside down. You know," he went on, changing the subject a little, "I cannot make out whether living in the East has made

me a believer or an atheist. Miracles in the style of the
Bible are simply day-to-day occurrences for me: I mean
here, when something exciting happens, there is always
darkness over the earth for three hours and the Rocks are
rent and all sorts of even better prodigies. They feel as
if these things happen, and in a sort of hopeless way they
do: for disentangling often means throwing the baby
out with the bath water." As Mr. Bristow lit his pipe he
began laughing again. "But as for the major part of the
story," he said, "I mean the spectacular years on the
banks of the Neva and the shores of the Black Sea—I
am afraid that part of the history is quite out of the
reach of your scientific scrutiny."

Here Mr. Bristow slightly underestimated my powers.
It was by discovering something about his Russian
adventures that I found out the truth, or something very
like the truth, concerning Balliol. Years after the conversation just recorded, during the war, a friend of mine
belonging to a famous family of old Russia was staying
with me in Teheran. He discovered that when Bahram
left Isfahan in his youth he took a Northern and not a
Western direction. He was educated along with one or
two other Eastern youths at a distinguished academy in
St. Petersburg, in which a group of Professors were in
intimate relation with a group of their Oxonian
colleagues. My friend's uncle was at that time the
honorary President of the Academy, and this gave him
the master clue in his investigation. (I need hardly add
that after meeting Bahram he became entirely absorbed
in the subject.) At some time or other in the 'eighties
some of the Professors of the St. Petersburg Academy
crossed over to England on a visit to Oxford, accompanied
by a number of their pupils. What happened when they
arrived at their journey's end can only be conjectured.
Their entertainment at Balliol was perhaps the most
striking of their experiences. Perhaps they met Walter
Pater at Brasenose; in the presence of these visitors from
the snows and the wastes he may have unbent a little, he

may have discarded the outward form of a retired military man and revealed the author of "Marius" and the custodian of the hard gem-like flame. Nothing is known except one tremendous fact: that the soul of a Persian boy was smitten with a love whose fire blazed on to the end of his days.

Although Bahram gave away the key of some of his mystery to my Russian friend, there can be no doubt that his delusion was a genuine delusion. It is difficult to insist on this point without raising the general reader's impatience, but the point is, nevertheless, the important one of the whole strange tale. I think I can do no better than appeal to an august authority. My subject is treated in a short story by Henry James, *A Passionate Pilgrim*. There an almost identical predicament is portrayed and the scene is the indentical ground of Bahram's wonderful dream. Oxford the sorceress forms the main subject of this fine flight of the master's fancy, and the "story in it" turns on a manifestation that the enchantments whispered from the many spires can and do actually cast miraculous spells over careless people, in the most literal fashion. Unhappily, as in so many Jamesian masterpieces, the great subject and the great handling of it lead only to a vast blank void. The reader, as usual, is left gasping in frustration like a landed fish. I wish that I could hand back to the master his subject as it was again shown forth in Bahram, with the addition of the great conclusion which he gave it. Rarely in the history of magic has an incantation worked wonders so finely and at such a distance.

Take the story of Bahram hitherto, cut it down to suit the prosiest taste, and it cannot fail to present a straightforward and neat succession of events: unusual talents, primrose paths, a fall, a redemption. As so often happens, real life then breaks in and spoils the design with clumsy and pointless elaboration. Shortly after my first meeting with him, Bahram backslid in almost as colourful a manner as he had surmounted his failings.

I like to think of Bahram in those halcyon days of
1931. (What halcyon days they were! Economic blizzards
blew round the globe, unemployment spread, Govern-
ments fell, income tax rose, and we thought we were
living through the climax of the modern ordeal!) He
was a very happy man. His friendship with Mr. Bristow
had recalled him to early ideals magically centred round
Oxford. He was reformed as far as reformation was
applicable to him. Although in moments of enthusiasm
he assured me that this was the case, his joys were not
attributable to the purity of his life or to intense religious
exercises. His moral sense, as any moralist would understand it, was quite non-existent. What Mr. Bristow had
done for Bahram was to salvage his virtues and cure him
of chronic drinking. No power on earth could have
weaned him further from his immense accumulation of
vice. He was a rollicking purveyor of all the forbidden
pleasures, and with that fantastical breadth of mind
which is endemic in Persia, he was fully conscious of the
preposterous contradiction between his disreputable ad-
dictions and his pose as a high-principled mystical
Dervish, without experiencing the least sensation of
moral dizziness. He indulged delusions as shamelessly as
other Persians indulge opium. And yet Bahram was not
a hypocrite. Perhaps the key to his odd enigma was this:
his virtues were as unusual as his vices were outrageous.
He had one very noble characteristic: he was loyal; he
was very loyal; and this in a country where that virtue
is hardly known and usually despised. If it were not a
tedious story, I would relate how Bahram once attempted
to save my life; as it is, I mention it as one among many
proofs. Well do I remember our first parting on the steps
of the Consulate General. "My dear friend," he said,
"you have made me as happy as a sand-boy, so called. If
I have occasioned you pleasure by showing you the
mosques of Isfahan you have given me equal pleasure by
recalling to me my lost youth and the green lawns of
Magdalen and Balliol. What I mean to say is: the

mosque of Shaykh Lutf'ullah may be unique, but so, as far as I am concerned, is that chapel at Balliol. *Mon Dieu!* What would I not give for a game of bowls on that lawn! God bless you." He burst into tears, and I was much moved. He may have been a little drunk.

Two circumstances brought about Bahram's second decline. First, his great friend and patron Mr. Bristow retired. This separation left a wound in his heart which the passage of many years did not heal. He knew long of the approach of this misfortune, to soften which he had begun, even as early as 1931, when I first met him, to seek familiar consolations. But the retirement of Mr. Bristow was far more than a personal calamity. It was a signal. A light went out. When he left, the Consulate General in Isfahan was closed. . . .

This may not sound very dreadful. Let me explain what it meant. In those days Persia was the scene of an utterly atrocious tyranny, only comparable to the extremes of totalitarian rule elsewhere. Now traditional British policy in the country was that of non-interference, and yet in a sense tradition had also made us interveners, made us the people to whom the Persians looked to modify the oppression of Reza Shah. Years ago we, the English, had gained for the Persians what civil liberties they enjoy; they could not believe that we would watch unconcerned while those liberties were destroyed. But we did watch unconcerned. It was an evil time; 1931 was the transition period. At that time the tyranny did not much worry an Englishman, nor Persians (like old Bahram) who were mixed up with the English. England was still respected and feared through habit. The process of our decline, however, was becoming noticeable to the Imperial party. Non-interference, they observed, was degenerating into a retreat before the all-powerful Anglophobe Emperor, Reza Shah. As yet this party had acted with caution, but they had their eyes on us, the weak wealthy ones, and on the sort of Persians who saw in England an ideal. Though nothing drastic had yet occurred, this trend of events was becoming obvious to ordinary people who lived in Persia. So when the Consulate General was closed, Bahram, like others of the pro-English party, knew what it meant: that England, the guarantor of liberty, was, indeed, as her enemies said, growing weary, and that henceforth they must stand up for themselves. The light had gone out. It was cold.

The second circumstance which tempted Bahram to a renewal of his follies was haphazard. A rich American, the representative of very great and important business interests, arrived in Persia accompanied by an astute and thoroughly "go-ahead" secretary whose position would be described to-day as that of his "Relations Officer." The main responsibility of the secretary was to see that his patron "got across." He considered that this trans-migration would be greatly assisted by a display of interest in the historical monuments of Asia, and he advised his patron to visit Isfahan and the ruins of Persepolis in the South. The rich American was obedient, and before long Bahram was conducting him round the ancient capital. The visitor, however, confessed to Bahram that, much as he enjoyed "rubber-necking in the Cathedrals," he had a keener interest in "gurls," that he would like to receive any available, "with you, Mr. Bahram," in some discreet and fully appointed house of entertainment. He had certainly applied to the right quarter. His desires were consummated. He had a further and less amiable weakness in which he liked to enjoy Bahram's moral support—namely, a cult of heavy drink-ing bouts. Three days after his arrival in Isfahan the American and Bahram set off to the South for the pilgrimage to the shattered opulence of Darius, King of Kings. They were picked up unconscious some three miles outside the town.

I did not see Bahram again till the end of 1933, when I returned to Persia with Robert Byron. As a friend of Mr. Bristow, he had in the meanwhile, come under suspicion from the Persian Government, so that soon after the closing of the Consulate he had found it politic to remove from Isfahan to the capital. This was a sign of the times, of bad times for any one so unpractical as to be an Anglophil. The retreat was now on. The passes had been sold; the oil, but nothing else, had been saved by luck in time; and our decline and fall were now accepted in Persia as a plain fact. Newcomers came on to the scene. The Nazis, ebullient, vigorous, young, already bloodstained, began to be hailed by Persians as their most likely saviours.

Can one blame those many Persians who transferred their faith to Germany? In Persia the Nazis pretended to be the champions of liberty. They pretended to be what we once were.

Anglophils became rare, our friends drifted sadly away; but Bahram, old, outrageous, monstrous, Hajji Baba Bahram, did not once falter. The whole "low" tone of his life became much lower than it had been in Isfahan—he had lost all his mainstays—but the principle which illuminated his life was never abandoned.

I met him shortly after I arrived in Tehran, that Tehran of thirteen years ago which I remember as a mass of wooden shacks and corrugated iron in the midst of which a large tiled mosque rose in ludicrous and pathetic protest. Robert and I had taken rooms in the Hotel Coq d'Or, a ruin in the Hafiz Avenue which was run by an amusing French couple, and I had not been there many days before stumbling footsteps on the stairs were followed one evening by a rap on the door, and Bahram stood before me. He stood there a while outlined in the dim light of the corridor, silent as though in deep emotion. Then shooting out his little arms, "as he would fly," he tottered across the room and hugged me in the Persian style. "Light of my eyes! Light of my eyes!" he gurgled in Persian as he buried his face in my waistcoat. "The beloved one has returned!" He was greatly

overwrought, and I knew that he was thinking of Mr.
Bristow.

The change in his fortunes was evident from his
appearance. The spruceness of his style of dress was
making little headway against his ragged poverty. The
ends of his sleeves and trousers were frayed, his suit and
linen looked dirty, and his face told a plain story of
much drinking. The habitual smile which I remembered
was replaced by a drawn look of anxiety, in so far as a
face cherubically round as his could ever be said to look
"drawn," even in times of bitter anguish. He no longer
looked at first sight like a Balliol graduate in a ski-ing
cap. He looked old, tired, and fearful.

Such was the first impression, and then his terrific
resilience obliterated it. There was a sudden reversion to
his old form. Before many minutes we were sitting down
chatting volubly about Isfahan, Oxford, England, and
the mass of common memories which we shared. His
smile returned irrepressibly. Waving his amber rosary
to and fro, he was soon in the thick of his anecdotes of
life in England.

"I remember well," he said as we moved to the tea-
table, "George Curzon saying to me once: 'Bahram, old
fellow, whereas to the Persians the sound of their sweet
language abroad affects them as a draft of sweet water
in the desert, so for Oxford men to meet in after life is
to halt the caravan and repose for a moment under the
spreading Chenar tree.' A most interesting fellow,
George Curzon; perhaps a little stiff and tedious at times,
a little formal for my taste, but a splendid companion for
all that. We were never very intimate. What I mean to
say is, Oscar Wilde was much more the type of man for
me. He was a great friend of mine. So was Mrs. Langtry."
When the servant came in he ordered a bottle of vodka.
He poured some into his tea. He drank three glasses before
he left.

Since his disastrous encounter with the rich American,
Bahram had relapsed into the character of a pathological

drinker. He did not often get drunk, but he drank with the methodical excess of the drunkard. Deprived of his former livelihood as cicerone of the mosques, he had become handy-man to one or two men in power, and did business for his friends the exiled Bakhtiarri Khans, who were then in the anomalous position of having been ousted from their feudal principalities and of being at the same time a considerable influence at the court which had subdued them. The reader will easily imagine what sort of services he performed for his various patrons.

There arose a certain difficulty in the way of our friendship.

"You know, my dear fellow," Bahram said to me one day, throwing himself into an arm-chair, crossing his little legs and dangling his walking-stick in a thoroughly English club manner of the old style, "under the tyranny of this bounder of a so-called Shah of ours I have to be excessively careful about seeing English people. Persians are not allowed, as you know, to speak to Englishmen. You did know that, didn't you? Charming state of affairs, isn't it? Very flattering to your Empire. I do not know what your Minister feels about it, but as far as I am concerned this situation is most painful, and dangerous too, as warm as toast, so called. I have endeavoured to ease it. I have explained to our invincible Chief of Police, General Ayrum—you may not know him, he's a wonderful man—a eunuch, with a beautiful wife and several children, and, believe me, a very great favourite at court; well, as I say, I have explained to this great national statesman, this bastard, that as an old Oxford man it is natural for me to drop into the Legation and into your hotel and so forth, in order to discuss University experiences with Mr. Mallet, and you, and Mr. Byron. But what I mean to say is, you might as well try to explain Professor Einstein's theory to a nightingale, and in fact the only condition on which I can see you is by acting as an agent d'espionage." Here he gave way to a long and most infectious chuckle. "So, I ask you to understand that you really must excuse me if I repeat anything I might hear about British policy to His Majesty's High and Imperial Government of Iran, so called." I caught the earnest look in his eyes. It was a valuable warning and I profited by it. To this dismal pass, to whispered warnings as to a wounded man in the enemy's path, Bahram's loyalty to the ever-radiant vision of Balliol had been reduced.

As the year drew to a close, and as the Persian scene darkened, Bahram began to sink further into the degradation from which Mr. Bristow had rescued him some eight years before. He was often drunk now, and, as drunkards do, he began to lose his sense of time. He was helping me in some historical research, for which purpose I had given him a rather valuable collection of papers which had come my way, when he suddenly stopped visiting me. For ten days I saw nothing of him, and when I sent notes to his hotel I got comical replies two days later. I began to grow worried about my papers, so one afternoon in December I went to his hotel. He was not there. He had left a week before. By chance there was a man in the courtyard, a horrible-looking vulture of a man, who said he knew where he had gone. "I'll show you," he said. I followed the vulture-man to an obscure caravanserai in the old mud-built southern quarters of Tehran, and there I found Bahram in company with a large number of bottles of vodka. The whole of one wall was covered with mathematical figures, and lurching about the half-ruined mud-and-plaster-built room, Bahram told me with a wealth of detail that he was working out "a most interesting alternative to the theory of spherical harmonics." During the ten or fifteen minutes I spent with him my friend drained a whole bottle. It was clear that not much time was left. I went and made arrangements with the American Hospital.

On the next day, a mournful snow-and-mud homesick Christmas, I remember, I went to Bahram's caravanserai in a droshky and removed him. He was still fully conscious. He must have had a constitution of iron. I left him at the hospital in the care of the doctor on duty. I had recovered my papers. I felt a glow of warmth at what I felt to have been my success in my own cause and that of Christian charity.

The next morning I received a note.

"MY DEAR FRIEND,

"Your kindness to me is most moving, and I shall always be profoundly grateful to you for having taken me to hospital. But last night I decided that this well-meaning scheme of yours was quite unworkable. My room was on the ground floor and so I effected my escape by the window.

"I have decided to retire to a Teheran slum, where I shall devote the few wretched weeks remaining to me, the most wretched of sinners, to drinking myself to death. Please do not try to find me. Please give my respects to Mr. Mallet, to Sir Reginald and Lady Hoare, and to their son, Joseph, who I am sure will grow into a perfect English gentleman, unlike myself, who was made for the filth and must return to it.

"Ever your grateful friend,

"BAHRAM."

My irritation at this neat legerdemain by Bahram at the expense of his good Samaritan was extreme. I immediately remade arrangements at the American Hospital and drove off in a droshky to Bahram's caravanserai, moved less, I fear, by indefatigability in the performance of good works than by the fury of hurt pride. I'd teach this Balliol buffoon to make a laughing-stock of me.

As I expected, I found Bahram in his caravanserai. Very mournful, sheepish, bewildered he looked as he sat there, dishevelled, and with a great goatskin coat pulled over his shoulders. It was bitterly cold.

"What the hell have you been doing, Bahram?" I said as I walked into the hovel.

"I'm waiting for a drink," he said tonelessly.

"You're waiting to be carted off by me, stuck on the top storey of the hospital, and kept there till you look like a human being."

This fine speech was interrupted by a ragged figure, who came in with a bottle of vodka and a glass. Snow was drifting through a broken window.

"Come on," I said to Bahram, "we're going."

He rose up to go. He was sober and without a will. He looked at me, beseeching sympathy, but I was affecting a very cold, grand manner. "Come!" I said, with a dramatic air of command, whose awfulness quite took me by surprise.

Bahram moved round the table to the door, utterly hang-dog. He paused and "One moment, my dear fellow," he said. "I will come, have no doubt about it. But, you know"—and he looked lingeringly at the bottle —"it seems to me that if you go to hospital to be cured of drunkenness you are expected to arrive—well, just a trifle 'bottled,' as we may say in English," and with a lightning movement he uncorked the bottle and stuck it to his lips. The ingenuity of the argument was so completely unexpected that I burst out laughing.

"Oh, all right, you old monster," I said helplessly, and, having drunk some of the bottle myself, dragged him away.

As we drove through the winter streets in my droshky, he fell once more into miserable sober gloom. We spoke little. He turned to me suddenly as we neared the hospital and said: "Whom do you prefer, Beethoven or Wagner?"

"Beethoven," I said.

As we drove in he said: "One thing I wish to say— one thing only. It is this. Mark it well. God damn and curse that great pimp H.M. the Shah-in-Shah of Persia, and, as *he* thinks, of Bahrein." They were fine last words.

I thought I had done a good deed, but I had done a foolish one. I should have considered more deeply the cause of Bahram's sudden steep descent into debauchery and hiding and made more careful preparations. For his violent breakdown was not merely an outburst of his lunacy, but of lunacy brought on by oppressive anxiety. I did not realise, and in his shattered state of mind he could not explain to me, that he had moved to a hovel in order to hide. Reza Shah was entering one of the first of his many fits of royal ferocity which terminated eight years later in near-madness. This mentally unstable autocrat had shortly before arranged for his friend and counsellor, Prince Teymourtash, to be tortured to death: he now turned in redoubled frenzy on Bahram's friends, the Bakhtiarri Khans, the Imperial favourites of the moment. Whole families were arrested and flung into jail; a large number were subsequently killed in the usual ingenious and diverting ways. Why this happened was never fully known. There was said to be a plot, but evidence was unconvincing: the friendship of the Bakhtiarris with English people probably had much to do with it (several of them had been educated in England); but the main cause was probably nothing more complicated than the normal hearty appetite for blood, particularly the blood of prominent possible rivals, which any healthy tyrant enjoys. This "purge" was in its early stages at the time of Bahram's entry into hospital. Two days after it was in full swing, and on that day the police arrived at the hospital and dragged him off to jail. I made as many inquiries as I could, but I could find out little. For his sake I had to be discreet. The prospect seemed as dark as it could be. General Ayrum, the acting Grand Vizier, hated him. Bahram was a man against whom it would never be difficult to trump up a charge: tyrants are always liable to be touchy about chastity. The chances that I would ever see him again were negligible, and the chances for him of a relatively painless death or one by torture were about even.

I considered him as among the dead.

It is strange how death throws life into perspective. The pattern seems indeterminate, until the end. I saw the career of my friend now for the first time as a co-ordinated whole, with its pathos, its poetry, its ungainly sequel. The moral was simple: If ever a man had lived too long, this was he. I liked that extravagant Persian miniature which he had fashioned in his mind out of his early experiences; and how gentle and touching the story would have been if Bahram, having made harbour at last, dreaming about Oxford and painting the adventures of his soul like the great impressionist he was, had died while under the influence of the one fine friendship of his life, while Mr. Bristow was still in Isfahan. His career, drawn out as it was in real time by real life, became disfigured by over-insistence on the moral lesson. That we are not such stuff as dreams are made on was the message bawled to the world by the example of his horrible ruin. There is no place in striving humanity for the unpractical æsthetician or the "escapist." Loyalties offered to beautiful delusions, especially delusions concerning values no longer in fashion, are counted as treason against marching progress, as blasphemy against the god of our day, the all-hallowed clock. If Bahram had forgotten Oxford, had consecrated his life to the chauvinism of his country and time, had sold his knowledge of England in the treachery market, he would have become a wealthy and influential man. He made a feeble attempt to unite himself to the spirit of his age, but he could not; he simply could not abandon the dream which had inspired him for so long. This crime was soon detected.

Lord Curzon might have been pained to hear that Persians were imprisoned on a suspicion of being Balliol men. Lord Curzon belonged to the past. Bahram belonged to the past. The world belonged to Youth and the eternal adolescence of dictators. That was the story, that was the moral of Bahram's career as set forth by real life, and, compared with the old artist of Isfahan, I, for one, thought she had made a sorry hash of the material.

Life, however, made amends. Having barged in, she continued till the whole was wrought into a larger and well-balanced work of art. The figure in the carpet was finally woven in full.

I heard nothing for more than a year, and I had long presumed that my poor friend had been murdered with so many others, when one day in Yorkshire I got a letter with Reza Shah's features on the postage stamp.

"MY DEAR FRIEND AND BELOVED,

"Mr. Summerscales has found your address and is sending this letter to you through the official Legation mail, the so-called Bag.

"Our beloved sovereign, H.I.M. Reza Shah Pahlevi, locked me up in his celebrated model Imperial prison of Kasr Kajar, as doubtless you will recall. After the passage of some ten months he graciously decided to permit my head to remain in my possession, and liberated me with a free and gracious pardon for whatever I had done to arouse his Imperial fury. This highly unexpected kindness of our beloved Sovereign has, if possible, increased my loyalty and regard for the throne and for its present august occupant.

"During my days of bitterness my worthy servant, a worthy descendant of Hajji Baba of Isfahan, removed most of my belongings into safe keeping, and to make them safer than ever he sold them to various worthy citizens of Tehran, who are preserving them with the very greatest of care. I am not, I thank God, a greedy man, but I miss my typewriter, the gift of our friend Mr. Bristow, particularly as I cannot buy another one for less than forty tomans. Your generosity is so great that I have no embarrassment in asking you for money. I do not state any particular sum. If you are wealthy, why, then, I should like you to present me with a large sum; if not, why, then, I recommend a smaller sum, and so on. You must adjust these disbursements according to your circumstances.

"You are very fortunate to be in England. It is far the nicest country in the whole world. Between ourselves, our own beloved country of Iran is a pigstye. Pray give my regards to Mrs. Montagu and to that charming young man, Mr. Rupert Belville, from their old admirer and your very devoted friend,

"BAHRAM."

For the next few years Mrs. Montagu, Mr. Belville, and myself ran a sort of "Bahram Benevolent Fund." I was the treasurer, and every year in March we used to send him a present so that its arrival should coincide roughly with the great Persian Spring Festival of "No Ruz," or New Year's Day.

What I chiefly liked about Bahram was his unchanging attitude towards Reza Shah. In the last few years enough has been seen and recorded of the degrading effects of tyranny, of its double-edged weapon of ferocity and seductiveness, to make any insistence on this theme necessary here. I would only remind readers that in those days, although the history of the world was always available for consultation, sensitiveness to the vileness and dangers of tyrannical rule was not very common. In the mid-thirties few things were more depressing to note than the increasing numbers of supposedly educated people, including eminent Europeans, who took to thinking and talking about the Persian tyrant as "this dynamic personality," "this forcible Sovereign," "this thorough and ruthless reformer," and such-like sweet nothings. But not so, never so, the old rogue from Isfahan. He saw through his savage ruler with beautiful clarity. I have often wondered which of two explanations to choose. Had Bahram caught some great and true inspiration from his visits to Balliol, and from his sojourn in the land of Pitt and Fox, which taught him to despise this hoax Napoleon? Or did he instinctively represent the most authentic and abiding virtue of the Persian genius in a high degree: that hard, carefree, hidden incorruptibility in corruption which has allowed the Persians to survive, almost as an intact people, the annihilating disasters with which their history is punctuated? Was he akin to the spirit in which a golden age of Persian poetry flourished under the barbarous Mongols? Either explanation meets the conclusion that Bahram was among the very few who never once allowed himself to be deceived by the glamour of that foulest of tyrants, Reza Pahlevi.

The war came and I lost all trace of him. Towards the middle of 1940 I was moved to Egypt, and used occasionally to be " called in" to committees who discussed problems arising in Persia. Our policy of the last fifteen years had yielded predictable fruit: the Germans were now accepted as the leaders of idealism and reform, while we were counted either as so far advanced in decay as to be powerless against the Emperor, or—and this was a more usual opinion—as the subtle, hidden, infinitely corrupt, and infinitely evil organisers of his despotism. The soil had been most perfectly prepared for a large-scale *coup d'etat*. In the summer of 1941 it looked as though a concerted rising in favour of Germany might take place simultaneously in Syria, Irak, and Persia. The magnitude of that threat, at that time, can hardly be exaggerated, and sober judgment to-day must attribute its failure more to German incompetence than to any inferiority in their political warfare and advantages. Perhaps throughout the countries of Islam Germans became deceived by their own deceptions: perhaps they thought that we were as totally incapable in war as we had appeared in peace. Then, as the summer drew to an end, a few hair-raising weeks reversed the situation to which we had grown used. Syria was wrested from Vichy, Irak was saved by a gallant few, and British forces marched into Persia from the South at the same time as their recent allies marched in from the North. In a matter of two days the imposing autocracy of Reza

Shah dissolved into dust. The old tyrant, now clearly insane, looted the houses in which he was sheltered on his journey to the South. As he left the country which he had efficiently organised and almost destroyed, he muttered to one of his friends: "I brought order here; I will take it away."

Throughout the period of these events I had been on a new planning committee in Cairo dealing with the Persian question. Amid a mass of names which I knew, the name of Bahram never made an appearance. This did not surprise me. He must be old now, I reflected, possibly dead. Just as well, I thought. I felt that years of pandering immorality must have so weakened his character that he would not now be able to cope with any fresh temptations. As to his loyalty, I felt uncertain and pessimistic. England is not remarkable for gratitude, particularly to the sort of friends and relations who offend her notions of decorum, and I had never heard Bahram express any views about the new German tempters of Persia. May God forgive me; I thought that it would be better if Bahram were dead.

At the beginning of October I was told that in view of my knowledge of Persia and Persian I was to be transferred from the army to work as a secretary in the Legation at Tehran. I bought some civilian clothes and hurried joyfully to my new post. Persia without Reza Shah!

For three days I hurried across those familiar deserts and uplands exalted with a mad illusion of home-coming. For the first time I saw those strange mixtures of chaos and continuing order which follow the downfall of despots. At every few miles on the road ragged bands of soldiers were returning from Reza Shah's two-day war. There was no police, no army; the few remaining officials were too frightened to use their authority, and yet, by ancient force of habit, I suppose, normal life seemed to go on as if nothing in particular had happened. The sweet voices of the Persian muezzins, the sweetest music of the East, echoed at the appointed hours in every town and village after ten years' compulsory silence. Tehran, I found, had been built anew at the cost of the last vestiges of peasant prosperity. A beautiful Persian town was standing where I remembered the corrugated iron of the 'thirties, and the large tiled mosque looked as silly as ever, and less now like a saving grace. The starvation introduced by Reza Shah continued.

It was as I was entering this changed and familiar Tehran by the Kazvin gate that I saw a sight which so took me by surprise that I uttered a shout before I realised what I had done. I stopped and stared. There could be no doubt about the identity of the round bustling figure walking down the Avenue of Sa'adi with the amber rosary and stick aflourish as I always remembered them. Bahram saw me too. He ran towards me. "Beloved! Beloved!" he cried as he embraced me, while the tears ran down his besotted old face. "How long is it? How long!"

"And what things have not happened?" I cried back. We were both moved. We were thinking of others who should have been there: Mr. Bristow, Robert Byron. Yet even as we greeted each other thus I felt my ignoble doubts returning. I could not help wondering why he looked so very well-off.

He had recovered all his old animation. His smile was as broad as ever, his moustache as dapper, his little figure not one whit less fat. I learned later that this resurrection was very recent. It had occurred with the entry of our troops. A panic-stricken Cabinet Minister had suddenly needed a friend at the British Legation, and Bahram suddenly found himself well clothed. But of this I then knew nothing. Two notable alterations attracted my attention: the Imperial ski-ing cap having been abolished, he now wore a broad-brimmed sombrero, and his grey hair, which had formerly been of moderate length and parted in the centre, was now close-cropped in the German style. I remarked on it at our next meeting.

"Yes, indeed," he said, passing a hand over his head, "I went to a barber in the avenue of the tulip-beds and the damned scoundrel of a teutonolator cut my hair short while I was asleep. What I mean to say is, that now that you have arrived, I will proceed systematically and methodically to grow it long again in the Oxford manner, for your honour."

He told me the story of his adventures during the war. They were well in keeping with the former Bahram legends. . . . I enjoyed this latest addition to the crazy comedy of his life, but it never occurred to me that here there might be a very great climax. Indeed, the possibility of their being any truth at all in the story of Bahram's "war effort" as related by himself did not seriously occur to me. Then a little later, quite unexpectedly and quite definitely, this possibility became evident.

It came about as follows. One day I was talking to a young Persian man, when the conversation drifted towards the subject of Bahram. He did not know Bahram, nor had he the least predisposition in his favour. So far as he was concerned Bahram was a well-known eccentric, wit, and pander, nothing more. When Persians are respectable, as my young friend was, they are quite indescribably respectable. He told me about Bahram's war effort. There was no difference in the two accounts at all. A vague suspicion then began to form in my mind that the latest passage in the saga might have more in it than at first appeared, particularly as my new informant had heard the tale, not as a piece of gossip, but from an eye-witness. I was anxious to meet as many Persians as I could, so I asked my friend to come to dinner and to bring his eye-witness along with him. I was careful to disguise my curiosity.

The eye-witness was extraordinarily shy. He had been clerk to the Press Attaché in the now disbanded German Legation, and he seemed to expect that I would bespatter him with recrimination and invective on this account. In order to ward off the blow he was at great pains during the first part of dinner, which was held on a beautiful blue-tiled veranda in a luxurious garden full of moonlight and the voices of nightingales, to inform me of the services which other people had performed for the Germans, comparing their iniquities with his own quite neutral work as a simple stenographer, typist, clerk, archivist, and confidential secretary. He was a tedious young man. I put it to him at first by implication and then by broad statement that I really didn't care a hang how blameless or otherwise his conduct had been, that I did not regard Persians who helped Germans as criminals, but as dupes, and that I was extremely interested in anything he could tell me about German propaganda methods and policy which, from his post in the press office, he must have been able to observe with much accuracy. I then began to eat caviar in abundance, having an as yet wholly unappeased appetite for that delicacy. The young man, meanwhile, droned on, telling me in much detail many things about German propaganda which I knew already, and nothing of interest. It occurred to me that he was not very bright or observant.

But he took heart at the fact, at last evident to him, that Germanophilism in Persia did not shock me, and this by degrees improved his conversational style. He dropped the rôle of informer, in fact he began to talk in a rather boastful fashion about the successes of the German Press department, with which, in a less and less guarded way, he associated himself. In the end he seemed to wish me to believe that he had been personally responsible for a great deal of German propaganda in Persia, while I murmured my congratulations. My interest, only kept wholly awake by self-discipline, did at last come to when the young man, towards the end of dinner, mentioned, as I had hoped he would, the name of Bahram, mentioned it in some disparagement. "He could have done a great deal," he went on, "but he is not clever. He is old, he drinks too much, he does not understand modern life. He is not clever." And then he told me of the incident which he had witnessed. It moved me to hear how Bahram's life, that weird mass of adventure, half-lost in delusions, half-lost in sordid horror, given design by a legend, was at its close crowned by the legend with glory. It is a remarkable story.

The German Press Attaché was one of Dr. Goebbels's most able representatives, and under his guidance German propaganda in Persia became an impressive monument to human ingenuity. It began with the question of Reza Shah, where the Germans found a curious advantage. Long before the days of Hitler, the Emperor, alarmed at his unpopularity, caused the spreading of a rumour that he and his great minister, Prince Teymourtash, were puppets of the British Government. The rumour was intended for a temporary emergency, but, unfortunately for its author, proved indestructible. It is still believed to-day. The Germans found it and kept it well irrigated. At the same time they let it be known that a supreme object of the Nazi career was the liberation of the Persians from their servitude. This explained for Persians why England and Germany were at war. Such was the foundation of their propaganda policy, and on it were built those pinnacled fairy palaces to the glorification of Adolf Hitler, whose wildest contradictions never seemed to diminish the faith with which they were believed, and whose immense success proved beyond the most extravagant calculation how deep is the element of fantasy in Persian character. By 1940 Hitler was accepted by the inhabitants of Persia, with passion and gratitude, as the following: the supreme Aryan; the leader of Islam and the hammer of all Christians; the Heaven-sent protector of Christianity and the drinker of Moslem blood; the great convert to Zoroastrianism and the revenger of this religion's sufferings at the hands of Moslems and Christians; the Mahdi; the last of the Imams; even as a direct manifestation of God; consistent only as the foe of Reza Shah. He was all things to all men. You took your choice. If you were zealous you were paid by the Press Attaché. Persians and Armenians, living in the same town, looked forward to the day of German victory convinced that each would be the other's slave. The Germans astutely gambled that no one, except English people, who would not be believed, would dare tell Reza Shah, who was disposed to admire Adolf Hitler, what was said about him through the secret channels of the German Legation. But though he had reared so tremendous a structure of falsehood, well adapted to the feelings of the people, the Press Attaché was not satisfied that his anti-English batteries had been built up to the full strength which the opportunity allowed. He wanted something a little less coarse and a little better reasoned, a little more deadly accurate for those few still unconverted Persians of Tehran who had been educated in English Public Schools and Universities. Someone whispered to him the name of the old gentleman from Isfahan. "He is poor, he is without principles," he was told, "and he, better than any one, can do it."

Bahram, at this time, had only a little recovered from his disgrace in 1934. He had escaped the death penalty by the exercise of his very considerable personal charm on his jailors and on a few men in power, but after his liberation he did not find it so easy as he had done before to find patrons. He was tainted by his former association with the Bakhtiarri Khans and with the English, and people feared to be seen about with him in a town supporting perhaps the largest population of informers of any capital in the world. He sank to a pitiable depth of poverty, earning his living when he could by the meanest and vilest services, mean and vile even by the standards of his wretched career as pimp and purveyor. He kept himself going by steady soakings in vodka and arak as much as by anything else. And then one day in the winter of 1940 there came to him the great temptation.

He was invited to the German Legation, and as soon as he arrived there he was ushered into the office of the

Press Attaché himself who received him personally and with marked consideration. Immediately, without ado, he made him a very large offer. He offered him a prodigious monthly salary, a luxurious flat, travelling facilities, a large car and chauffeur, everything! And he presented these delights in the most seductive manner known to the powers of darkness. He appealed to his finer feelings. The Imperial tyranny, he said, under which the people groaned, and under which no one had suffered more bitterly or less deservedly than Bahram, could only be cast off with foreign aid. Only one foreign Power was now prepared to make common cause with the defenceless partisans of liberty in Persia, and that Power was Germany. He wished to enrol Bahram as a soldier in the common struggle. Did he agree? Of course he must agree. And what was he required to do? Here the Press Attaché put forward his proposal with the utmost delicacy. He took Bahram into his confidence. The first thing to do, he explained, was to clear the ground. People must be detached from loyalties likely to confuse the issue. He knew well Bahram's feelings about England, he could understand them; he himself had once been, he went on with moist eyes, a very, very great admirer of England: he was not likely to forget his happy student days in one of the great Midland cities, nor his happy afternoons at Simpsons, nor the Regatta at Henley. But that was England as she was, whereas—now? He shrugged his shoulders. The Jews, he whispered, the Freemasons, the decadence. . . . He raised his eyes for a moment. He then leaned across his desk and fixed Bahram with a steady blue gaze. "It would be a great thing," he said, "if you would accept a position as a writer of leading articles in a paper, as I can arrange. I would like you who know England so well to tell your countrymen about the great future they would have with us as allies. You understand? All that we have discussed this after-noon—I would like *you* to tell them."

I have no doubt that Bahram could have modestly

enriched himself by keeping this proposal in negotiation and suspense, and I would not have much blamed him if he had. But in the utterly incalculable way of Persia he recognised this occasion as sublime, and he rose to the height of it; more than that, indeed, he magnificently over-topped it. At the supreme moment of his life Bahram stood up and uttered these words: "I am surprised that you are so foolish as to make such a suggestion to a Balliol man." In sudden fury at such insolent words from a disreputable old pauper, the Press Attaché leaped to his feet. Bahram laughed in his face. And then he waddled out of the office, out of the great glossy pompous hall of the Legation, and disappeared again into his dim, hated, familiar world of brothels, poverty, cold, hunger, and hard-earned drink.

That is the end of Bahram's story. There is little to add by way of epilogue. He was drinking pretty hard when I saw him again. The Russians had arrived, and Bahram, not without profit, had constituted himself into a sort of unofficial entertainer and introducer of the Allies who, at that time, had precious little other means at their disposal of meeting one another. The Russians set him off on another reckless career of drunkenness, and I had to organise another cure. I never heard of another relapse, so perhaps this cure was final. One of the few deeds of my life on which I look back with unmitigated satisfaction is that, after learning the true facts of Bahram's war career, I obtained a pension for him from the British Government. It was not a large pension, and I gave a perhaps slightly misleading account as to why Bahram should be considered eligible for one, but I obtained it for him, and I have never had the smallest pang of conscience about those technically misappropriated funds.

3

ROBERT BYRON

That man who knows, and who knows that he knows,
Is like one mounted on a horse which can overleap the
    arch of the Heavens !
The man who knows not, but knows that he does not know,
Will reach the same place in the end astride his halting
    pack-beast.

HAFIZ.

I FIRST MET Robert Byron in 1926, when I was a fresh-
man at the University; he had left at the end of the
term before I arrived. In contrast to the custom of
public schools, the "old boy" is not a familiar character
of the Universities; Oxford considers herself to be a
sufficient, self-contained world, and any sense of being
a stepping-stone to a greater world beyond is re-
markably absent. "Old boys" (the term does not figure
in Oxford slang) are members of colleges up for a week-
end, and no prestige attaches to them. There are, however, exceptions, of which Robert was a striking one;
for he had belonged to a great Oxford period, the period
which non-Oxonian *Punch* portrayed with popular in-
accuracy for years after its cessation as a town populated
by æsthetes in flowing hair in perpetual strife with
exasperated athletes. It was, in truth, an outlandish
Oxford enough.

Attempts have been made to evoke the fusion of
ancient tradition and what was then ultra-modernity,
which made the quality of mid-twenty Oxford, of which
Harold Acton was the Arbiter Elegantiarum, and Robert
one of the prime movers, but the only truly successful
description of this remarkable phase of University life is
to be found in the opening chapters of Evelyn Waugh's
novel, *Brideshead Revisited*. People may believe that in

this book he cannot be attempting a serious picture of that ancient seat of learning, but the picture is true.

As suddenly as this world of fantasy had leaped into being it vanished. The Michaelmas term of Autumn, 1926, came round, and Oxford was the old, pleasant, unique, but mainly humdrum place it had been before. But the legend lingered on. It lingered on not only in repeated tales of the wonders that had passed but an instant away, but in a survivor of the great age, in Harold Acton's younger brother William, whose rooms glowed solitarily like the last fierce blaze of a once-widespread conflagration. Every Saturday he entertained a host of fellow undergraduates and celebrities to a lunch of lobsters and champagne before the weekly hunt with the drag-hounds, and on many evenings he set even more lavish entertainment before even greater numbers of guests. It was here that the past generation of Oxford reassembled from time to time, and in William Acton's rooms there was enacted the rarest of all human dramas— a successful revival of dead golden days. It was here that I met the famous figures of the great Oxford past (time at Oxford still has the mighty dimensions of childhood), among whom was the subject of this essay.

Robert changed little in appearance during his life. When I first met him he looked older than his age, at the end of his life he looked somewhat younger. As I try to recapture my first meeting in my mind's eye, I see little difference in the figure of that young man of twenty-one and the friend to whom I said good-bye fourteen years later. Only in one respect was Robert's appearance extraordinarily changeable. He became fat or thin with great rapidity. If he got what he wanted to eat he became fat in a matter of days, if not, he lost weight immediately. I seem to remember him first in a festive, crowded, smoke-laden room, as moderately fat, short, with very fair hair, a penetrating rolling eye, a face of distinction, somewhat like that shown in portraits of the Bourbon kings, and a voice whose quiet lazy intonations never concealed the abounding vitality behind it, and which, on sometimes small, and sometimes not easily detectable provocation, broke out into a violent spatter of invective. Someone told him I was a Roman Catholic. "Oh, God," he burst out, half-rudely, half-jokingly, "I thought we were going to become friends." But we did become friends notwithstanding.

I have said that in Robert's case the law whereby the "old boy" cuts a small figure in Oxford life was suspended; even undergraduates, those weary men of the world, could not easily resist a high degree of curiosity about a frequent visitor bearing the name of Byron, who had travelled in little-known parts of Greece, and who had written a book about his adventures which had received some serious attention from reviewers. Alone in our rooms we gave way to a good deal of clandestine admiration.

I met him several times during my University career. It would never have done to have said so, or even to have hinted at such a thing in urbane Oxford, but I felt honoured and excited that he should have sought me out. He told me that he was studying material for a work about Eastern Europe, and he wanted to read my father's books on the Ottoman Empire.

He often used to come to my rooms in Peckwater when he was on visits. The three-year difference in our age was a strong difference. I tried desperately hard to be adequately clever and amusing. He told a friend of mine that he liked me, but that he sometimes found my conversation intolerably obscure. I once dined with him at the "George" in company with a Greek whose English was a little less halting than Robert's Greek. Robert explained that this was his Greek tutor. A large, pale undergraduate walked in. "Who's that?" Robert asked. "A German," I answered, "I know him quite well. He's a very interesting man." Robert turned with a shudder to the Greek tutor. "Don't you loathe foreigners?" he said. "Don't you think everyone except the English and the Greeks are absolute hell!" The Greek tutor agreed politely.

In London, Robert had a flat near Bryanston Square, where I sometimes used to spend an evening with him. We knew many of the same people and used to meet at parties both of the respectable and unrespectable kind. Our friendship was not an important part of either of our lives, but it was a pleasant part. The difference in our ages soon became psychologically negligible, my conversation was growing less obscure, and we amused each other immensely with tales of our foreign adventures. Delight in travel has for long been an English characteristic, but among the young men of the 'twenties the cult became an obsession. We were both obsessed strongly. But I did not suspect then that for Robert foreign travel was part of an immense design of life. He was a gay young man, apparently living for pleasure and writing articles and books by way of occupation. He rarely spoke seriously about these things in my hearing. When his second book, *The Station*, came out in 1928, I read it with surprise at the gravity and scholarship which it displayed.

In 1931 I came back from Persia, and our real abiding friendship began. It came about like this. I returned to London in the middle of the night, and, having the wrong address of my sister's house, I ended up, after a long hunt for lodgings, at the Savoy Hotel. The restaurant was closing, and as I arrived a group of friends walked out into the street. They were Harold Acton, Desmond Parsons, John Sutro and Robert. My homecoming was celebrated with drinks in my room. Before we parted, I arranged to lunch with Robert the next day, as he wanted to have a long talk with me. We lunched at his club and spent the afternoon together. He asked me whether on any of my journeys I had gone as far as Central Asia. I told him that I had been on the Turcoman Steppe, which is technically in Central Asia. He asked me whether I had seen any large brick towers of great antiquity. I described to him all the towers I remembered seeing in Persia, drawing pictures of them and of designs of brickwork which I remembered from them. He did not seem satisfied. He told me that he had seen a book while in India illustrated by old photographs of Asiatic buildings, and that he had been particularly struck by what seemed to be tall cylindrical brick structures in Northern Persia. There was one of these towers, free of much ornament, which from the photograph appeared to be one of the great buildings of the world. It was reputed to stand on the Turcoman Steppe. As we talked on in the December afternoon he explained to me the reason of his strange curiosity. While in India, from which he had returned the year before, he had studied, as far as his time allowed, Indian architecture. While he admired many of the great Moslem monuments, he felt that they had a certain air of unreality about them, as though, in many cases, the impressive marble and precious materials in which they were wrought were often hiding an uneasy sense of sham. He had felt a similar sensation when looking at Islamic monuments in Turkey and Egypt; as though, I remember him saying, he was looking at a picture of a building and not at the building itself. He had been led like others to the theory that a central impulse of Islamic art was to be found elsewhere than in the places he had visited; in Persia. But when he came to study Persian architecture he had met these unexpected photographs of brick towers. "What the hell are they?" he said.

At the end of our long, extremely interesting conversation I was left with a disquieting feeling that while in Persia I had not used my powers of observation, of which I was becoming rather proud, as well as I might have done. He said that in the next year or in the year after he hoped to be able to go to Persia. Perhaps we might go together.

It was shortly after this renewal of our friendship that I discovered for myself, tardily enough, that Robert was a considerable writer. He had just published a small book called *An Essay on India.* I had read a review of it in Cairo on my way home. The critic, I remembered, had treated the book with severity: here was a young man, he said, who had knocked round India for a few months and then set up to lecture the world on that vast subject. Doubtless, if he could find the time to pay a more protracted visit, etc., etc. One had the impression that the critic had spent a large part of his life in India, and could have written a much better book on the subject had he chosen to. I now read the book myself. My impression then was the same as my impression now, that it is one of the best books written on any Asiatic subject by an Englishman. To me, then, with a mind made busy by experience about the relations of Europeans and Asiatics, to read this extraordinary record of observation and criticism was a profoundly exciting experience. The book, I have found in the course of years, bears a classic mark of excellence. To read a few sentences at random in any of its many descriptive passages brings, in a sudden onrush of recollection, the feeling, the sights, the sounds and the smells of the East vividly before the mind.

It is always exciting to discover that a friend is more than merely intelligent, that what we assumed to be normal polish and brightness is in effect the gleam of rare distinction. In Robert's case a sudden discovery of the dimensions of his mind and character must have been experienced by many of his friends. Although he could be very self-centred on occasion, even disagreeably so, there was little egotism and no vanity in him; in his literary character, though not in other ways, he was a very modest man. He took elaborate pains to perfect his literary talent, but he never regarded himself as the outstanding writer which he became by his last book; he never regarded himself as in the least unique, and when he found, as he did several times, that he was doing valuable things which no one else was doing, his first mental reaction was not a pardonable one of pride but

rather of indignation that important work was being
neglected. He never spoke about his writing with the
faintest trace of self-satisfaction ; indeed, when he
mentioned his books, which was not very common, he
usually did so because the reference was essential to the
argument. He generally assumed, sometimes with
comical results, that everyone he met was as intelligent
as he was and better educated. This modesty, which was
in contrast to the fiery enthusiasm of his convictions, was
so very marked that I can well imagine him to have had
unliterary friends who never knew that he had written
a single book.

From 1931 onwards Robert and I saw much of each
other—that is to say, we saw each other frequently on
the rather infrequent occasions when we could; we were
both such slaves to the habit of travel that there were
big intervals when geography divided us. But his
suggestion, made the day after my return home, that we
should go out together to Persia in search of brick towers,
though it did not much tempt me at the time, did in fact
lead to our travelling together for a year. We went to
Persia, Afghanistan and India during 1933 and 1934. The
result of this journey was Robert's last and best book,
The Road to Oxiana. I am the "Christopher" who is
frequently mentioned therein. I shall always feel proud
that I helped him in the composition of one or two
passages; and though the description of me unhinged
with terror in a forest which occurs on page 260 is entirely
libellous, I find abiding joy in being so closely associated
with that classic of travel-literature and art-history. To
read it is, for me, to relive the most enjoyable experience
of my life, enjoyable for the marvellous variety of distant
lands and human character which the journey enabled
me to study and for the companionship of that man.
Before discussing Robert's character, however, and our
travels together (for my vision of him is bound up with
memories of those adventures), I would like to attempt
an appreciation of his literary career which may be said

to have terminated with the publication of the *Road to Oxiana* in 1937.[1]

His first book, called *Europe in the Looking Glass*, was published in 1926. It was the first of the four travel books he was to write, and he was fortunate in choosing for his first appearance a form to which his talents were easily adaptable. He was twenty-one when he wrote this record of a journey taken with two Oxford friends to Germany, Italy and Greece. Later, when Robert was a mature writer, he looked back with shame on this first effort, indeed he kept the memory of it so dark that, though I had discussed his writing with him very often, when I came to re-read his books after his death I found I had wholly forgotten the existence of this one. Youthful indiscretions in literature are paid for by years of regret, by horrible delusions that they are frequently re-read aloud amid derisive laughter, by weary pilgrimages to the libraries of one's friends with the object of theft and destruction. Robert suffered all this in the acutest form, but reading this slight, gay, youthful production of high spirits, I find nothing of which a good writer need later have felt ashamed. It stands up, indeed, with surprising assurance amid the serious productions of his full-grown talent. There are, of course, passages of youthful *naïveté* whose juxtapositions with the extraordinary precocity of other passages strike unintended discords; but this almost inevitable fault of young writing is very amply compensated by what I find it easiest to call a certain steadiness of purpose which keeps the high spirits, the comedy, and the enthusiasm in some control. Robert grew up quickly. *Europe in the Looking Glass* might easily

[1]To assist the reader I give a bibliography of Robert's main productions:

Europe in the Looking Glass	1926	*The Appreciation of Architecture*	.	1932
The Station . . .	1928	*First Russia Then Tibet*	.	1933
The Byzantine Achievement	1929	*Innocence and Design* .	.	1935
The Birth of Western Painting	1930	*The Road to Oxiana* .	.	1937
An Essay on India .	1931	*How We Celebrate the Coronation* .		1937

Among his most interesting writings there was also an essay on American Public Opinion written in 1939 for the Foreign Office. No copy, however, appears to exist in the archives to-day.

pass as the production of an older and less talented man.

The book is extraordinarily interesting for the way it illustrates the consistency of Robert's mind. The sense of humour is recognisably the same as in his later years, chiefly characterised here by a delight in the grotesquely and portentously female.

"A woman"—this from a description of a hotel in South Germany—"had sat next to us at dinner in a dress of brown tussore, printed with green and yellow boxes in perspective, so that she might have been covered with angular warts. These danced before my eyes long into the night."

Of Nuremberg he says:

"The buildings convey the same impression of affectation as the baronial rafters of the Queen's Hotel, Margate."

Of Florence: "There is nothing so pleasant as revisiting . . . Florence, when the monuments . . . are no longer weighing on the conscience."

A reader who knew Robert at any time of his life will recognise the peculiar tang of his humour in these quotations from a book written when he was little more than a boy.

His observation is already abnormally acute. With very little study he disentangles the elements of complex situations, and is rewarded at one point by a lucky guess (I think it would be romantic to rate it higher) which turned out to be a prophecy exact in detail. Of Bavaria he says: "It is here, more than in Prussia, that the survival of militarism is to be feared." But the greatest points of interest in this first book are the recorded beginnings of his interest in Greece, an interest which never left him; and the stated purpose of the book, which was, in fact, to be the purpose of his life. It is the presence of these passages which indicates the consistency of his mind.

Robert's surname was not, as he sometimes told gushing admirers, related by nothing more than coincidence to that of the great poet. He came of the same family, from a branch which sprang from the main line in the seventeenth century. When he arrived in Greece he was welcomed as a representative of the most honoured name in modern Hellas. "To avoid . . . self advertisement," he says, relating his first Greek adventures, "I may admit at the outset that all Greeks feel a personal pride in meeting a person bearing my name." He was moved, and remained profoundly moved throughout his life, at the loyalty and gratitude which so distinguishes and beautifies the modern character of Greece. This impression largely formed the direction and the pattern of his subsequent career, and beginning, as his career did, with an act of gratitude to his family, his impetuous nature conceived it as his duty to repay a debt of honour by continuing the Byronic struggle. Robert was a fighter by nature. The phase of the struggle which he determined to open was the vindication of the great neglected Greek heritage of Byzantium. He entered the world of Byzantine scholarship with a war-cry.

Of Byzantine study, which was to become one of the main interests of his life, there is only bare indication in this first amateurish and carefree book. But there is one passage, at the beginning of his opening chapter, in which he strikes a deep note of seriousness and in which he sets forth his aim in the world. I give the passage in full, not as an example of Robert's prose (he was still a long way from mastering his powers of expression), but as showing the fullness of his self-knowledge and determination even in the bewildering period of early manhood.

"To attain a sense of the relative proportions of the various entities of which the modern world is composed, it is essential clearly to define the position of the United States. This is only possible by comparison with Europe. But Europe, taken as a whole, is such an unknown quantity to most of its inhabitants, nurtured in the disastrous tradition of the armed and insular state, that they are unable to gauge the contrast between their own corporate civilisation, the laborious construction of two thousand years, and the retrograde industrialism sprung up in a night on the other side of the Atlantic. Admittedly it is not to be expected that the doings of three young men, interpreted through the pen of one of them, can prove of any serious value. But if, in providing to a certain degree, however lop-sided, a picture of the continent of which England forms a part, those doings will further in any way the new sense of ' European Consciousness ' that is gradually coming into being, perhaps the reader will forgive the incohate agglomeration of trivial fact and irrelevant opinion, that comprises the remainder of this book."

Robert not only held hereafter to the aim expressed in that passage but enlarged it greatly: to understand, as far as it is humanly possible to do so, the whole world into which he was born. The enormity of this ambition is less remarkable than the distance he travelled towards its realisation. He began the understanding of Europe by the study of Greece. To understand Greece he went to Mount Athos.

In his second book, *The Station* (published in 1928), he records his experiences, and analyses briefly the life, the psychology, and the art of that incredible and now almost vanished survival of another age, the Holy Mountain. This is how he describes his immediate purpose:

" . . . While the classical continues to suckle half the world on a voice of letters and stone, one fragment, one living articulate community of my chosen past, has been preserved, by a fabulous compound of circumstance, into the present time. Thither I travel, physically by land and water, instead of down the pages of a book or the corridors of a museum. Of the Byzantine Empire, whose life has left its impress on the Levant and whose coins were once current from London to Pekin, alone, impregnable, the Holy Mountain Athos conserves both the form and the spirit. Scholar and archæologist have gone before, will come after. Mine is the picture recorded."

This passage is typical of Robert. The boldness and decision of his imagination, the breadth of evocation, the self-confidence without the morbid self-consciousness of the period in which he was writing, and the spirit of hostility to the classical tradition which he conceived (too extremely) as the enemy of Christian Greece, are all characteristic. Equally, the very imperfect use of metaphor (". . . suckle half the world on a voice," etc.) remains unfortunately frequent in nearly all his early writing. I shall speak later about Robert's style, which, in contrast to the rapid development of his mind and his ideas, conserved such blemishes right into his maturity. His aptitude and his literary aims were occasionally at cross purposes, and this retarded the full flowering of his gift of expression.

Robert's major gift as a writer, particularly as a recorder of travel and an evoker of history, was his ability to enter states of mind which were foreign to his nature. In the following passage he comes near to impressive accuracy in describing the inspiration which gives life to the monastic ideal, not only on the Holy Mountain, but in all religion. In reading this passage it is necessary to remember that its author was at the time not only an atheist but an active, vigorous enemy of the churches to whom the conventional practices of religion were stultifying misdirections of energy. (Later in his life he became not only more tolerant, but near to being a conventional Christian.)

The paragraph preceding the one I quote gives

statistics indicating the extent of the monastic population
of Athos throughout the ages.

"It will be seen from these statistics that the
Mountain is no mere coccyx on the body politic of
Europe but an organism in which the germs of life
are as vigorous as when first implanted. And it may
be inquired, of what nature is the attraction offered
by the cloister to the man of the twentieth century?
The cynic, the materialist, and he who boasts his
common sense, will reply: Indolence and shelter. Nor
will they be wholly at fault. But their perception is
not acute. Institutions are not borne flourishing
through a thousand years on such ideals alone.

"In the composition of man there is body, there is
reason; so with the animals. And there is something
further, which the animals do not share. This, the
essence of all true satisfaction, takes the form of a
quest. In some its impulse is negligible. In others it
dictates the whole course of existence. Of the latter there
are, in the main, two sorts. There are the humanists,
who hold to the fulness of living, whose faith rests
implicit in the virtue of the earth to set the seal to
their desires. For them their Absolute is inseparable
from that alliance of the physical and transcendental
which the language terms Beauty. And, secondly,
there are those for whom no physical interpretation,
no channel other than the direct, can suffice. These are
the religious. . . .

It is clear that for the first, the humanists, religion
will frequently mean nothing; and that in no circumstance will it conjure in them the fundament of
emotion that it does in the second. But it is the tragedy
of contemporary transition that for the second, the
instinctively religious aimed towards an Absolute
external to the earth, there exists, in many cases, no
religion adequate to the direction of their imaginings.
Thus it happens that in both . . . there has arisen no

mere negative distaste for Christianity, but an active detestation. This is born, for the humanist, of the belief that religion of any kind degrades man by directing himself from himself; for the religious, of the canting phase and withered fable, beneath which, as memory tells him, the emotions of childhood were stifled and unpicked.

To approach those humorous and kindly men, the monks of Mount Athos, in a temper of psychological understanding, it is necessary to forswear, if only temporarily, the sting of these prejudices. Let the humanist realise, atheist though he be, that the religious seeks ... the same as himself. ... And let the religious who is agnostic visualise to himself another Christianity, far different from that which has been extended and distorted through four centuries of uncongenial logic; a Christianity not yet moulded by Latin materialism to the convenience of an institution; not wrung by civil wars, combed with the burrowings of sectarians, and balanced between the parties of the state like a boulder on a needle; but a single path of exploration, unclouded by doubtful ethics and hieratic blackmail. . . . Such was the Christianity that conquered, and such, on the Holy Mountain, it has remained."

In this spirit Robert searched for the soul of Greece. With his three companions he visited the many monasteries which cover Mount Athos. The resulting book is a curious production, difficult to classify. The loose and elaborate construction makes it rather heavier going than others of his books which were designed for a more specialised audience, and the reason is probably to be found in the fact he was still very young, hardly twenty-three, and that he had not yet obtained control over his immense cleverness. The book is at once a history of the monasteries of Mount Athos, a lighthearted record of a journey, a description of men and landscapes, but with these elements confused together. His power of selection was as yet unformed, it was still drowned in his eager enjoyment of life. I calculate that the book is about forty pages too long, and that if Robert had revised it and reconstructed it ten years later he might have made of it something imperishable. As it is, rather than a good book (I am applying the standard of his masterpiece) it is a book full of astounding flashes.

The growth of his ability to describe is what these flashes reveal most immediately. In the following words he describes a sunset, recalling the account of the Mountain, which he quotes, written in the fourteenth century by Sir John Mandeville.

"I turned to go. But stood, rooted. For there, out upon the water, moving with an impetus almost visible up toward the cold lowering horizon, lay a grey elongated cone. The shadow: which ' rechez unto Lempny, the whilk is therfra nere lxxvii myle.' Slowly it was dissolved in the approaching night. A film crept over the peacock rim."

The quotation has already occurred in the book, and re-enters naturally. Note how completely this purple passage is free of sentimentality. There are many such throughout the book.

Robert was an admirable comedian, and his comic gift is present in most of his books, but surprisingly enough, his humorous writing, like his style, developed slowly. His early books are often marred by joking passages which must strike many readers who never knew him, who cannot imagine the intonations of his voice, as meaningless. Like other writers of his generation, the exaggeratedly sophisticated humour of mid-twenty Oxford probably contorted his sensibility for some time. In his full maturity he developed a remarkable and impeccable technique of humorous writing of which several portents appear in *The Station*.

A conversation with a young monk.

"... He turned to me and said: 'I am a man of the world.'"... He began again: "A few years ago a man died here who had a number of medals ..."

"Medals?" I replied, not wholly understanding the word.

"Yes, medals," he repeated, drawing imaginary ribbons on his chest. "When you return to England, will you send me some?"

"Send you some medals? But how, and for what reason?"

"Why not? Can't you go to the Foreign Office in London, and have them sent to me?"

"But why? You have done nothing."

"No, but I will. I will do great things. I love England."

"But you must do them first. Besides, the Foreign Office does not distribute medals."

"The Foreign Office does not distribute medals? Who does?"

"The King."

"Have you visited the King?"

"No."

"I visited our king three times." Pause. "But when you get back you will send me those medals?"

"No. ..."

"What can I do to be famous? I do want to be famous."

Another conversation:

"We bathe every day, Father Stephen. Are there sharks here?"

"Sharks? They abound."

"Have you seen them?"

"I? No, I haven't seen them. But there are quantities."

"But if you haven't seen them, how do you know?"

"How do I know? They ate a deacon two hundred and fifty years ago. A lamb was set as a bait; they caught the shark, and there he was inside."

These passages in his very best vein of comedy remind a reader of his later work, but they are jostled among some youthful obscurities.

Robert's belief that the spirit of Byzantium lived on in Athos vigorous and authentic was unquestionably a true one. In the later chapters of his book he first expresses his views on the nature of that Christian Hellas which, possibly as a distant result of the odious conflicts of the Latin and the Eastern worlds, has never till recently been admitted by Western scholars to have been an ennobling or important contribution to the content of civilisation. Once again Robert proves in his early writing the consistency of his mind: the ideas he formed of the nature and significance of the late Roman Empire and its heritage remained with him throughout life little changed. As the views which he expressed in *The Station* are the same as those which he elaborated in his next two productions, I will not discuss them for the moment except to say that they were deep and right views, but coloured, as they remained, as much by his antagonisms as by his admiration. He could not express his love for modern Greece without launching an assault on the rival West, particularly on the Roman Catholic Church for having condoned the treacherous attack of the Crusaders, and on dons, schoolmasters and scholars, for belittling Byzantine Greece in their worship of Antiquity. I would not have had him different. There is something extraordinarily exhilarating in all his work on the Byzantines. He was the champion of Constantinople against all-comers, even against the ancient Greeks themselves, but it is unhappily not possible to deny that emotion often confused and diminished the abiding value of his judgment.

While his polemic career as a Byzantinist is wholly

foreshadowed in *The Station*, there is another shadow too of the future. El Greco is mentioned several times, and the opinion is recorded that the great Cretan "was a Byzantine artist of the strongest conviction," and that in his life's work he "brought Byzantine art to its logical fruition." El Greco's Byzantine ancestry in art is now admitted by every critic. At the time Robert was writing, this view, though it had already been put forward, notably by Strzygowski, was not widely held. Conservatives still looked upon it as a fantastic extravagance. The later work of Robert and his friend Professor Talbot Rice (one of his companions on Mount Athos) was largely responsible for the fact that to-day El Greco is naturally accepted as a great Byzantine, that this is now no speculative theory but a part of educated mental furniture. But Robert's strange and in some ways grotesque excursion into art criticism belongs to a later paragraph.

The next year, 1929, when Robert was still very young, only twenty-four, his first important book, *The Byzantine Achievement*, was published. The book has a peculiar origin. Let me quote the record of Professor Talbot Rice, his companion in Greek travel:

When Robert Byron first went to Greece in 1925, his interests lay in the field of world politics and international questions, and on reaching the country, he at once became immersed in Greece's problems, brought at that time so vividly to the fore by the recent expulsion of the Greeks from Asia Minor in face of all that had been decided to the contrary at Versailles, and by the burning problems of what to do with a million or more refugees, for whom there were no homes, no work, and no food. But as he travelled through Greece, something new happened to Robert. He fell literally head over heels in love with Greece; some very moving descriptive passages in *The Station* and *The Byzantine Achievement* bear witness to this.

The Byzantine Achievement was the direct outcome
of Robert's leading interest and his new emotional
experience. In the first place he at once saw that
Greece's political problems were not to be explained
simply by a survey of events from the beginning of
the 1914 war, or even from the time of the War of
Independence onwards. In the second his analytical
mind demanded some logical explanation of the
emotions he experienced as he looked at Greece's landscape and imbibed her air. Greece's beauties were for
him not to be explained by her ancient history; they
were not centred around any sentimental love of the
classics or any deep admiration for the sculptures of
Præxiteles or the lines of the Parthenon. Yet, he felt,
there must be something more to account for the
intensity of his love than landscape and climate alone;
the atmosphere of history and the past must have been
present in some form or another. One object of *The
Byzantine Achievement* was to show what this was.

After an introduction dealing in turn with *The
Historian and his Problems*, *The Greeks*, and *The Byzantines*
—the preliminary inquiry into his emotions—Robert
turned to a fuller examination of what he termed "the
anatomy of the problem," and it is here that his ability
as a writer and his penetrating powers of analysis were
first given full scope. His chapter, "The Triple Fusion"
contains perhaps the most successful synthesis of the
problems of the origins of Byzantine culture that has
so far been attempted. Rome, Greece, the East; the
stable, the cultural and the transcendental; these are
the elements that he distinguished as the basis of
Byzantium.

Robert's full aim here was to write two books: *The
Byzantine Achievement* was to be the first; the second,
which was never written, was to have been a history of
the contemporary Eastern Mediterranean. He never
abandoned the idea of his second book, and when I last

heard him speak about it, some two years before his death, he had enlarged his original intention to writing a history of the First Great War. I cannot imagine, however, that had he survived the second war he would not have made another change of subject.

As it is *The Byzantine Achievement*, "An Historical Perspective," as he calls it, is the only example of Robert's work as a historian pure and simple. As I shall explain more fully later, he did not believe in the "historian's detachment." He declares at the outset that he writes as a partisan, with a "pride, a patriotism in our age." He wrote as a fighter against the age's enemies, and the first victims of his wrath were those same professors of classical learning whom he had already mercilessly knocked about in *The Station*. In his second chapter he charges into battle.

"The travelling pedagogue, who admits the existence of the native population only to lament the absence of that vacuous perfection which he conceives to have been the Hellenic physiognomy, will maintain an opposite opinion." (That the modern population of Greece is in the main racially identical with the ancient.) "But it is doubtful whether, amid his texts and annotations, he has ever acquired sufficient acquaintance with human character to divest his heroes of their heroics and discover the men beneath. Those, however, who have drunk the humanities as a medicine rather than an intoxicant, will recognise in the modern Greek mentality and temperament the counterpart of the ancient."

This is excellent. But what spoils the book is that these attacks occur so often that one gets an occasional impression that he is pelting professors for the sheer fun of it, and also, as in *The Station*, that he sometimes considers an attack on what he dislikes equivalent to exposition of what he admires. This is all the more regrettable, as even at this early stage of his life he was such a masterly contriver of positive effects in writing, as the following description of Greek character makes plain:

"The salient and most permanent impulse of the race is an avid curiosity. The zeal for knowledge, which inspired the first philosophers and the first scientists, differed in no way from that to which St. Paul, in an age of new necessity, cast the bait of the Unknown God. To-day the "men of Athens" still greet one another with the words τί νέον what news? and await an answer. In the country a regular [formula of personal interrogation is the preliminary to all hospitality. There results from this insatiable attitude of inquiry, a universal, and to the Briton, extraordinary, respect for learning, for books as books, and for any aspect of cultural ability. From the highest to the lowest, even to the illiterate, this national trait has endured through the ages. And, as might be expected from an acquaintance with either the Ancients or the Byzantines, history is regarded as a recreation rather than a study, the leading newspapers exhibiting daily columns from the pens of its foremost professors.

"The perpetual dissatisfaction with the outward semblance of things also engenders, as it always did, a depreciatory clarity of vision. The Greeks, in contrast with the English, are lacking in that quality of self-deception which so assists a moral people in its dubious enterprises. Though capable of untruth in pursuance of an aim, with themselves they are honest. They employ fact in both speech and literature, to the detriment of those decencies which Anglo-Saxons prize above truth. And it is to this exercise of semi-cynical semi-satirical insight into the weaknesses of human motive, that they owe the genuine, passionate spirit of democracy which they translated into political science, which was the foundation of the Byzantine monarchy, and with which they are still imbued. Through 3000 years Greek history exhibits no vestige of a caste system. The pedestals of popular esteem are, and always have been reserved for men of learning, servants and private benefactors of the state, and occasional families who have enjoyed a record of public service through two or three generations.

"It is not, however, to be supposed that the Greek is inquisitive only in the manner of the savage. He is gifted, in addition, with a uniform standard of intelligent ability, such as characterises, for instance, the Jew." (I omit a passage comparing Greeks with other Balkan people.)

"Save when an opportunity for actual participation in the affairs of the state presents itself, their discussion constitutes, without rival, his national recreation. Those who have moved among the English working classes testify unanimously that their interest in politics is aroused only during the transitory excitement of elections. In Greece, so alive among the obscurest grades of society is the tradition of every man's partnership in the conduct of the country, that parliamentary government is rendered almost impossible, unless supported by the steadying loyalty that attaches to a throne. This latter the Byzantines possessed ; while the popular vice, argument, was diverted to the less destructive province of theology. To-day the political recrudescence of this vice is focused in countless newspapers, whose acrid party columns vividly recall the petty states and infantile wars of the classical era. But, beneath the surface currents of recrimination, there flows a deep religious patriotism, a mystical faith in the Hellenic destiny, which is fundamentally different from the chauvinist imperialism of the West. Corollary of this is an insane party loyalty, which can agitate the domestic life of the country to an inconceivable degree. In both national and party causes the Greeks are indefatigable propagandists. Hence, in these spheres, truth is often elusive. Similar tactics in business dealings lead them to excesses, which those whom they outwit term dishonesty and double-dealing. In this connection, however, it is impossible to discount the effect of four centuries' misrule and insecurity, from which a large portion of the population has not been twenty years delivered. . . .

"The people are devoutly religious and devoutly superstitious; though their aspirations of soul have never been systematically diverted to the purposes of an institution by the exploitation of superstition, as in Latin countries. Towards nature, flowers, trees and birds, they feel a romantic, almost spiritual love. This, owing to its having attained widest expression in the writings of antiquity, is often termed pagan as though it were in opposition to Christianity.

"Finally, and most essential clue to their character through the ages, the Greeks are imbued with the same conceit as they ever were—a conceit so cosmic, deified, part of the order of existence, that outward expression of it is superfluous and its ultimate discovery leaves the stranger with a sense of shock. European neither in fact nor feeling, they talk of ' Europe ' as somewhere else, and regard foreigners, though with tolerance and sometimes affection, as lacking in those essential qualities which have always constituted the Hellenic superiority over ' the Barbarians.' This conceit renders them impulsive and, therefore, physically brave; it also deprives them of sound judgment in moments of crisis. Since the War of Independence they appear to have been inspired with a singular devotion to Great Britain, which originated in gratitude and has been maintained by the Greek appreciation of the element of justice in the British character. If proof of their constancy in friendship be desired, it is forthcoming in the fact that, despite the events between 1914 and 1923, this feeling has remained.

"Such in retrospect and present fact, is the Greek character. A clever, conceited and inquiring race, intensely political and intensely democratic, reserved in its friendships, conservative in its beliefs, commercially gifted, responsive to the emotions of nature and religion, the Greek people has endured, poised between East and West, child of neither, yet receptive to both. Originally an alloy, it stood like a new metal, bridge from Africa and later Asia, to carry North-West the foundations of a world civilisation. This work accomplished, it has preserved the identity of which that world then strove to rob it."

How much of this makes poignant reading to-day! The main thesis is a contradition of Gibbon's conception of Mediterranean history, that the events of the Empire after the death of the Emperor Marcus were a continual process of decay, a conception which, if taken seriously, can only explain the fact of Constantinople and the duration of her Empire from antiquity to the fifteenth century as a stupendous inanity. Robert believed, on the contrary, that the Byzantine Empire was the high noon of Hellenic greatness. Is his thesis a true one? Does he illustrate the truth of his belief? Let me answer by quoting Professor Talbot Rice once more:

"The story Robert Byron tells is no mere historian's controversy; it is a record of the facts, as they are available to us to-day, and it brings out clearly the true nature of the age, one of periodic renewal and rebirth in art and culture alike. Even if the size of the Empire was reduced, the quality of its cultural life remained, or was even enhanced. Byzantinism was something basic and vital in Europe. 'Whether applied to man, spirit, institution, or work of art,' he wrote (page 76), 'it denoted nor East nor West. It is an adjective apart, exclusive yet cosmopolitan, austere yet delectable. But in its whole composite significance, two elements predominate: the Christian and the Greek. Without this alliance the universal civilisation of the West could never have evolved. And it is this alliance, whose personality, tested to the depths of human suffering, has survived in the twentieth century.'

"This broad culture was the outcome, to some extent, of Byzantine social institutions, and Robert goes on to show the nature of these. That there were some bad rulers in eleven hundred years was inevitable, but in the main the conduct of home affairs was surprisingly fortunate, and the population of the Empire probably enjoyed greater freedom, greater opportunity, and a more advanced culture, than any other body of people in the world, certainly before, and possibly even since. The Empire, he shows, was no whim for successive rulers to toy with, as were so many Empires of the early East and the more recent West; it was an institution run for the good of the people, and in which every opportunity was open. This view, accepted as a matter of course by many writers to-day, was less obvious only twenty years ago, and Robert's role in changing our comprehension of an age in the world's history has been very considerable."

The most striking passage in the whole book is contained in his eighth chapter, in which he discusses the art of the Byzantines. Of this chapter Professor Talbot Rice says as follows:

"The long chapter on art in *The Byzantine Achievement* is no less penetrating. 'The function of art,' Robert wrote (page 171), ' is to translate the philosophic emotions evoked in the artist by the inner significance of material objects, into visible and ultimately intelligible form.' And this function, he sought to show, was more fully exercised throughout the Byzantine age than at any other period. 'There developed,' he wrote (page 197), 'a definite cubism in drapery and in natural phenomena, such as trees and rocks; a contrasting shiny darkness for the accentuation of face and limb; and a treatment of celestial portent not in the familiar physical terms of mediæval domesticity, Renascence beatitude or baroque tornado, but geometrically, in compartments whose very simplicity of outline is alone compatible with the pent reservations of the artist's feeling. To this skeleton of representational formalism, colour gave the flesh, colour employed not merely as an adjunct to the modelling, but fired with an independent life, so that its so-called light and shade derived not from some fancied external source, but from an intrinsic virtue born of its own interplay. And there emanated, from this combination, an expression of mystical emotion to which the modern mind is even yet scarcely capable of responding.' As a definition of Byzantine art this passage has not been surpassed. But when Robert wrote it, it seemed as if a new age, the equal, even the culmination, of Greco, was to be born. That modern art has fallen so short of the ideal is one of the tragedies of the years between the wars."

The last paragraph brings me back to an important characteristic of Robert's literary psychology: his enthusiasm for his age, an enthusiasm which he did not qualify till much later. I have already referred to his "patriotism in our age." In gross forms such patriotisms, involving allegiance to "New Orders," "dynamisms," and so on, are familiar. Now Robert's patriotism was removed from any such crudities; he was deeply concerned for the honour of his times, but whereas to most men such honour seems remote from obligations, to him detachment here was treason. His whole attitude in this was instinct with nobility, but also instinct with error: an error in emphasis on the value of time necessarily implying a belief in the sanctity of modernity. From this there sprang some failures of reason and vision, not altogether surprising in a man of such fiery temperament to whom objectivity was never easy, but which would have been less surprising in a lesser man. The result in this book, in which he presents a reconsideration of the Byzantines as a modern need, is that he occasionally falls into the very error which he castigated in the classical pedants. His patriotism leads him to excesses of praise and blame.

This comes out most strongly in his views and treatment of one subject, which, as we always disagreed on it, I might have preferred not to discuss, but which I cannot leave unmentioned (although I am a partisan in the matter), as, of his many prejudices and convictions, this was one of the few which remained with him unchanged till the end of his life. The subject was Roman Catholicism.

The destruction of Constantinople by the soldiers of the Fourth Crusade in the thirteenth century was as detestable as any crime recorded in history. Pope Innocent III sought to prevent it, and denounced it when it had happened, but, most unhappily for his and the Vatican's reputation, he condoned it later. The effects of this stupendous disaster have been long-lived. It made a final chasm of hatred between Greek and Italian, and between the Greek Orthodox and Roman Catholic Churches, which has never been bridged, and perhaps never can be bridged; while in the Eastern Mediterranean of to-day the bitter feud continues. It is not unconnected with the hostility between Russia and the West. Inevitably Robert caught the infection of this strife, and inevitably he took the side of the Greeks. As strongly as he was attracted by the beauty of the Christian Greek conception of life and the world, that diffused and tolerant mysticism which adorns Greek life with strength and beauty, as strongly as he championed these neglected marvels of the world, he was repelled by the harsher, more matter of fact conceptions of the West, which he saw, in their evilest aspect, embodied in the Roman Catholic Church. He saw the Vatican as a sort of ball and chain attached to the West preventing escape from all that was degrading, uninspired, and calamitous, in the European past.

In the gradual realisation of his ambition, to obtain a comprehensive understanding of the world into which he had been born, he greatly modified many of his views. I know that later he bitterly regretted the intemperate violence of his language about ancient Greek art and the Renaissance, but on the subject of the Roman Catholic Church, he remained uncompromising. After his death I often wished that he had seen Catholicism at its very best, in the conduct of the French clergy under the German occupation, and in the undeviating courage of the Catholic hierarchy in Germany. I often thought that these manifestations of the very soul of Catholicism might have altered his view, but on reflection I doubt it. Like Luther, he was convinced, I believe, that the Papacy was identical with Antichrist. The heroism of the Catholic faith in adversity would, I think, have seemed to him only tragic. As he grew older his hostility lost its narrow character, he withdrew credence from some time-honoured old wives' tales, never again did he write with the same violence on the subject as he used in *The Byzantine Achievement*, but the hostility remained to the end as a prominent part of his character.

Yet, even to a reader who is occasionally shocked by his extremism, *The Byzantine Achievement* is an enduring and beautiful book. In his brief and masterly biography of Gibbon, Mr. G. M. Young recommends it to any reader who wishes to correct the error of Gibbon's bias. Robert suspected that this was overpraise, but it was not. He well deserved it. His chapters on the Religion and Culture of the Byzantines, his description of "The Joyous Life" of Constantinople, his unfailing insight, and his emotional description of the fall of the city, and the beautiful diminuendo with which the book closes, are all of them pieces of writing of such strength and perception that they become part of a reader's mental possessions.

The Station is the brilliant performance of a brilliant young man, a book redeemed from youthful faults of construction and imperfectly controlled cleverness by remarkable passages; *The Byzantine Achievement* is much more. The leap to maturity is formidable. It is essentially a fine book. It marks Robert's entry into the world as a made writer, and it is always surprising to remember that he was under twenty-four when he wrote it. He was not a case of precocity; he matured quickly. "I was never adolescent," he once said to me. "I cannot remember ever being younger than I am."

At this point in his career his development remained more or less stationary for a time. I say "more or less," because among the books he produced between 1929 and 1933 there is one, his *Essay on India*, which stands out with his last book as one of the best productions of his life. But with his other books, though the standard of writing is maintained and the insight is as revealing, circumstances for a time impeded any radical growth in his stature. One reason for this was that with his increasing facility he sometimes wrote too quickly. He was always a painstaking writer, but in order to write at his best he needed to write extremely slowly. For this, in a life made busy by the immensity of the tasks he set himself, he could not now always find time. Another reason, I believe, was that he made a grave error in the choice of his material at this stage. With his violent and combative nature he was ill-fitted to become an art critic, but this is what he now became in the book he produced with his friend David Talbot Rice, *The Birth of Western Painting*.[1] It was completed in 1929 and published in 1930.

This book is Robert's last production of his Byzantine period. His aim is to indicate how the Byzantine tradition was the origin of European painting, and how that tradition finally flowered in the genius of El Greco.

I feel that it is only honest for me to say that I have

[1]The whole text of this book was written by Robert Byron.

no liking for this book; that I regard it as a serious error, and cannot believe that its main contention is conceivably true. I know nothing about art, I attempt no serious criticism of the book in detail, but there must be a ground where ordinary acquaintance with pictures and specialised knowledge meet, and on this ground I find the book, from the point of view of art criticism, full of such fantastic exaggerations and preferences as to be at times monstrous. I believe that Robert met here with a familiar calamity: that he had a great subject and important ideas to lay before the world, and that in the first flush of enthusiasm he flung his subject and ideas into a work before the maturing process had been at all completed in his mind. He might have written his greatest book on this theme. As it is, the myopia of enthusiasm and of his ferocious partisanship lead him into grotesque assertions, of which this, on his second page, is a typical example:

"Times have been when artists have fallen to accepting the natural world without inquiry and reproducing it. Such was the misfortune of Antiquity and, with the exception of the French impressionists, of Europe from the sixteenth to the nineteenth centuries."

On the fly-leaf he quotes the famous jibe of El Greco at Michael Angelo: "He was a good man, but he could not paint," and throughout he offers the suggestion that the achievement of Renaissance Italy, of Northern Europe, of England, and pre-impressionist France, may be dismissed as so much wonderful nonsense and no more; Greco was the one truly great artist between the fall of Constantinople and the first modern painters. I believe that any respectable authority on art must regard the expression of such opinions as a grave aberration of talent.

Had Robert limited his aim, had he called the book "The Byzantine Ancestry of El Greco," or by some such title, then he might have made it worthy to rank with his finest work. Yet as it stands, as an expression of a mood, as an assertion of a passionate admiration, the book, if you forget its title and its generalisations, is convincing and exciting. As in *The Byzantine Achievement*, Robert is a great companion within Constantinople, when he forgets his irritation with the world of the West, and is in the genial company of his beloved Greeks. His second chapter, for example, of forty-six pages, in which he outlines the origin and the extraordinarily beneficial results of the Iconoclast controversy on Byzantine Art, is among the best things he ever wrote, and to the general reader, if to no other, is extremely illuminating. Once again, Robert displays his remarkable ability to penetrate a very different state of mind to his own. He once told me that the greatest mental exertion he had ever experienced was in trying to explore the attitude to life of the Iconoclasts, and that this attitude never ceased to perplex his imagination. Both here and in *The Byzantine Achievement*, where he first broached the subject, he appears to me to succeed abundantly, both as a scholar and as an imaginative recorder of the divagations of the human spirit, and, without being fantastic, I believe it is possible that the intense aversion which he felt at this time to the whole achievement of representational art (which includes so enormous a part of European art) was due to the fact that in studying the Iconoclasts of Byzantium he became influenced by their beliefs. His thesis is, in brief, that the art of Antiquity, surviving in the representational and degenerate art of the Græco-Romans, was so inadequate to the aspirations of Christian monotheism, and also presented so definite a temptation to a relapse into idolatry (the then chronic weakness of the Eastern Mediterranean), that it excited a Christian iconoclasm in Constantinople on the model of those frequent iconoclastic movements of the Semitic world recorded in the histories of Jewry and Islam; that the impulse to art was too strong to be repressed, and that the unlooked-for result of this iconoclast movement was "a compromise, of austere and unearthly magnificence, whereby the artist, in place of reproducing a subject in the exact likeness of his world, was now to reproduce his own emotional reaction to the central and One Factor in his and everyone else's lives."

As I can make no claim to any special knowledge of Byzantine studies, I add a note supplied by Dr. Otto Demus of Vienna University.

"It is very difficult to classify Robert Byron's Byzantine work as his books do not belong to any of the usual categories. He might be best described, perhaps, as a geistesgeschlichtler, a recorder of the movements of mind and spirit in the past. His facts, except as regards Philosophy, are usually second hand and acquired by a great deal of reading. He is always honest about this, he makes no pretentions. He seems to have taken Strzgowski, Millet, Diehl and Meier-Graef, an unusual collection, as his main guides, supplementing what he took from them by his own erudition, which was considerable, sometimes astoundingly so, though sometimes noticeably incomplete. On several occasions he boldly interprets the dates of works of art by his own feeling for style rather than by an analysis of evidence, as when he quite correctly differs from Millet as to the date of the chapel of the Prodrome in Karyaes ; but as a rule he accepts the results of others unquestioningly. For all that his work is that of a pioneer.

He appears to have been attracted to Byzantine studies on two accounts, both related. The first (the origin of *The Byzantine Achievement*), was the study of contemporary affairs in the Eastern Mediterranean which led him to study their historical foundations. The second, which drew him to Byzantine Art, was also an interest in the present: in modern French painting.

"In the field of painting, he found in late nineteenth century painting a quality of 'Colour Relation' and interpretational form which he associates (as Cezanne and the Fauves did themselves) with El Greco and through him with the art of Byzantium. Here, as elsewhere, he becomes unjust to other phenomena in order to underline those values and movements for which he had an enthusiasm. It is noteworthy that he not only quarrels with the European Renaissance ' the alien tradition ' as he calls it, ' which, though it created the most beautiful works known to man, became no more than a prison whence it has taken Western European art five centuries to escape,' but with certain periods of Byzantine art too, the Justinianic for example, as when he speaks of the figures in the Justinian panels of San Vitale, as being ' not composed but ranged . . . like ninepins.'

"*The Birth of Western Painting* is not very well constructed; the two parts, the analysis of Byzantine painting and the chapter on El Greco, are not well balanced. The first part has many good things, especially his discussion of Iconoclasm where he shows not only great perception but sound scholarship. His chapter on Greco is not so impressive although his contention is sound. Strangely enough, proofs of Greco's Byzantine ancestry are more abundant than he supposed. Paintings signed by El Greco painted in a rigidly Byzantine style exist. Whether El Greco remained so wholly and so consciously Byzantine throughout his career, as Byron insists, is open to question. There is no suggestion of his later style in his early pure Byzantine work.

"Taken as a whole, I admire the freshness, passion, and curiosity of his Byzantine books. Byron saw and stated problems often overlooked by the specialist. The defects of bellicosity did not prevent me from getting great pleasure in re-reading them. They embody the adventurous spirit of the author, and of his times, and he clearly had an inborn feeling for colour, a rare thing in Byzantine studies, which is a game usually played by colour-blind elderly gentlemen with bad photographs."

I may have seemed unduly harsh on *The Birth of Western Painting*. Let me say that though I disagree with it, even dislike it, I sympathise with it, and greatly respect the experience of which it is a strange but sincere expression. I have been told often enough that without visiting Spain it is impossible to understand El Greco. I cannot, therefore, pretend to have "seen" his works. I have some notion, however, of what the experience may be. During the war I was stationed near a country house in Scotland where there are two of the greatest paintings by El Greco in existence. I used to visit them frequently during four months. I found that, though I am not in any extraordinary way sensitive to painting, these pictures began to haunt me. I became unable to banish the thought of them from my mind. My visits multiplied, and memories of other great pictures began to grow less precious, in a disconcerting manner. I remembered Robert's extraordinary book. I do not think that any one with any knowledge, even the barest, of El Greco has the right to look down on an obsession with the work of this greatest of artists. People who develop such obsessions should be respected and envied, for they have drawn near the dazzling truth.

1929 was a very important year in Robert's life. It marked the end of his first period in which he had devoted his early manhood to Byzantine studies. *The Byzantine Achievement* was published in this year, *The Birth of Western Painting* in the next year, but he had finished the writing of it by the summer, and his mind was ready for new adventures. At that moment he had a stroke of good fortune. He was offered an opportunity to work in India for eight months,[1] and the by-product of this experience was one of the best books he ever wrote: *An Essay on India*, which was published in 1931. It is an astonishing production. I believe that the late Lord Willingdon's opinion that this was the best brief statement of the modern problem of India was no overpraise. It would be well if all young men and women going to India for the first time were to read this short, wise description of what awaits them.

It can best be described as an appeal to common sense against the racialism of English convention in India; though the book contains much else, this is its constant and important theme. In this book Robert stated his main ideas fairly, without rancour, without intemperance. He had probably begun to regret the violent invective which had marred his Byzantine work; he had cleansed his bosom of much perilous stuff, though, unfortunately, some of that perilous stuff remained to leave a blemish here and there. Total pacification of such a violent man as Robert was not to be accomplished quickly.

The book is simply and well designed in three parts: he calls them The Problem, The Indians, The English. I can do no better, I think, than to quote from these three parts to illustrate the quality of the book, and the development of his central idea.

The following are from "The Problem."

On page 4 he records his reasons for writing the book:

"My sojourn in India was a period of acute intellectual strain. The strain began as I stepped from an aeroplane at Karachi on August 4th, 1929; and it by no means ended as I boarded a P. & O. at Bombay on April 4th, 1930. . . . I had never felt, nor wished to feel, any interest in India. Now, having returned from

[1]Robert's aim, in which he succeeded, was to visit Tibet. He obtained his fare to India from Lord Beaverbrook in return for articles describing the England-to-India Air Mail. After his return from Tibet he found he needed to earn money to return home. He obtained employment in an oil concern in Calcutta through the good offices of a friend.

India, I am burdened with thoughts that give me no peace and have destroyed the harmony of my former way of life. The burden is not one of responsibility; I neither feel, nor desire, a mission to humanity. My worries arise because it seems to me that the outcome of the present problem between English and Indians can determine the character of all future civilisation. I see the whole philosophy of Western history and culture, already thrown aside in Russia and the United States, undergoing the supreme and ultimate test of its practical value. And if I say selfishly that without this philosophy the world will be no place for me, it is because, in so saying, I reflect the opinion of that small minority within the small enclave of peoples in Western Europe, with whom alone rests either power or will to preserve the diminishing sanity of the race against a barbarous and rapidly expanding materialism."

This, on page 13, is from a passage where he discusses the sudden total preponderance of the West during the nineteenth century in the hitherto gradual evolution of contact between East and West.

"But it is not only a question of needs, of cheap Lancashire cottons, or a supply of kerosene in the village shop. It is a question of the moral effect of the first train, the first motor car, or of the first aeroplane. If a swarm of strangers arrived on us from the moon furnished with aerial torpedoes at moderate prices, and then converted the summit of Everest into a hive of industry, we ourselves should feel inferior, and wish to reform our way of life in accordance with the new methods. Thus it is with the less advanced peoples. Factories arise, and with them a building of enormous fortunes, whose success depends, not as formerly on the mere exchange of goods, but on their production in quantity. The indigenous industries become absurd. Labour flocks to the cities built by Western enterprise in Western fashion, receives higher wages than before, and gazes with awe upon the interloper's vast system of organised amusement. The native inhabitant may approve, may disapprove, or may, as in the majority of cases, simply accept the situation; he also may make a fortune, or he may remain a scavenger impervious to all hope of advance; but whatever his opinion, condition, or success, his surroundings are calculated to inspire him with an irrevocable sense of inferiority, and often, if he has enterprise, with a wish to emulate not only the qualities that have brought material success to the Westerner, but his most insignificant and ridiculous mannerisms. Thus baseball has become the national game of the Japanese, and the Indian Congress party must needs invent a flag and national anthem."

In the succeeding passages he contrasts this sense of inferiority with the arrogance which it has aroused in the Westerner, the arrogance not only of success but of a superstitious emotion that white skin confers divine attributes. He then moves on page 20 to a recollection of his arrival in India in order to illustrate the extraordinary novelty, both material and psychological, which the arriving Englishman must meet.

"As I stepped from the aeroplane . . . the gaze of the crowd turned . . . to my hat; so that the following morning I hastened to buy a topee. Its presence on my head, together with the sahib-formula of address . . . induced a sudden feeling of unreality. . . . I saw myself as a Russian film-producer would have seen me, badged as an Englishman-in-India, a brutal imperialist. . . . I tilted the topee uneasily.

"Karachi groaned in silence beneath an English Sunday. The taxi moved leisurely down the main street, skirted a clock-tower encrusted with Gothic pinnacles, then swerved into a tortuous lane. Silence and Sunday were gone. A hive of humanity beset us, chaffering before the open-fronted shops and booths, hurriedly removing their persons, chairs and pipes . . . lest our progress should be impeded, idling, contemplative, or hastening on errands, bearing loads, chattering, begging, rescuing their children; but one and all turning . . . their eyes in our direction. Without purpose or interest they gazed, and their gaze was the only static element in a cauldron of mobility. . . . Inside me was something very, very strange. For here was I in a position which I had never conceived or wanted, a ruler among the ruled. . . . It was written on every face, and if mine proclaimed a doubt, the topee hid it. . . . I was disquieted, and my companion noticed it. . . . ' Look at them,' he said. ' It makes you realise what we're up against here in India.' It did. It made me realise that the thing we are up against existed in myself."

He states the problem briefly in these terms: that the English in India have, in material and political experiment, gone farther to achieve a beneficient contact between East and West than any other machinery of Empire; but that the Englishman, by assuming racial superiority, has embittered against him the people he has benefited. English traditions of personal dignity are assimilated by Indians and increase the friction. The English must recognise that many of the problems which afflict them are of their own making, and that they alone can and must make amends.

The second part, in which he describes the people of India, is divided into four sections: an introduction; the Ryot (or peasantry); the Princes; and the Intelligentsia. In his introduction he demolishes (but quite gently) the foolish idea that no such entities as "India" or "the Indians" exist. He points out the profound truth that the integrating principle in India has, throughout recorded history, with few exceptions, been that of conquest by foreigners (at present we are the integrating

principle: we have integrated, for example, the Army of
India and Congress), and that in contrast to this there is
a disintegrating tendency which he associates (possibly
romantically) with the climate and landscape. He moves
to the subject of the Indian peasantry:

> "The traveller in India, and, for the matter of that,
> the educated resident, English or Indian, seldom leaves
> the ordinary channels of communication. As the motor
> traverses the main road, or the train flashes through
> the eternal scene of little fields and ditches broken by
> the sharp blue-green of parky trees, he looks from the
> window and then leans back again, knowing that India
> is all and always the same. Sometimes the tower of a
> temple, sometimes the dome of a mosque or tomb, or
> the outline of a ruined fort blurred with pestiferous
> creepers, breaks the horizon, to recall the activity of
> remote individuals. But the recollection is dissolved
> as the motor draws up to refuel, or the train to re-
> water, by the uniform stares of a seething humanity
> born out of nothingness, to gaze for a moment before
> expiring into nothingness."

The whole of this section of the book, a reasoned
statement of the position in the world to-day of the vast
unpolitical mass of peasant India, is filled with passages
of admirable description from which I have chosen the
above as being of quotable length. He outlines the
formidable subject of Hindu-Moslem antagonism. He
notes its political and psychological aspects.

> ". . . The religious genius of India finds its truest
> and oldest expression in Hinduism; and one suspects
> that the continued vigour of Moslem belief is largely
> a psychological reflection of the Hindu's ineradicable
> theism and consequently of the desire for differentiation
> in that respect. The traveller in India, beholding for
> the first time the towering temples of Dravidia, or the
> artistry impressed on every stone of the Black Pagoda

at Kanarak, begins at length to grasp the universal dedication of the people. But in buildings the traveller is living in the past. To discover the reality of popular religion in the present he must look about him, must observe the habits of his servant or such daily sights as that of a pipal-tree growing from under the foundations of a neo-German office next to the Calcutta Stock Exchange and daily refreshed with small offerings. Then by degrees other and more dramatic incidents will obtrude upon him."

I find the following, from page 70, in the section on The Princes, extremely illuminating.

"The English are fond of indulging a theory of the Princes' inalienable devotion to the King-Emperor and the Queen-Empress, whose signed photographs occupy the place of honour in every palace drawing-room, and whose wooden portraits executed by Indian copyists poison the meals of every palace dining-room. This devotion is simply that of a lesser royalty to the fount whence he draws his royalty, his stars, his guns, his manners, and the pattern of his court. Thus used the Byzantine Emperors to invest Balkan princes with the uniforms, privileges, and the title of Cæsar. In modern times, the British throne is the last great fount of sovereign dignity; and lesser sovereigns, as long as circumstances allow, will be unwilling to loose their connection with it. . . . Once their royalty is assured, the Princes are first and foremost Indians, as sensible of the white humilation as the rest. . . . Were an independent India to offer greater assurance, for an independent India they would work, and would undoubtedly prefer to work. At present this is not the case. But it may become so."

He defines "The Intelligentsia" in the last section of "The Indians" as

"The whole of that broad class throughout India whose minds have been trained by Western education . . . and whose conception and ideal of progress have been borrowed from the West. This class . . . is the voice of India. To the contention that it is unrepresentative of India, many irrefutable arguments may be addressed. But it is India's only voice."

Though excellent as a guide to India and the Indians, this book has really one subject: The English in India. He considers peasants, princes and politicians in relation to us, the integrating force. It is this, I think, which largely gives the book its excellence: able, as he was, to see foreign or unsympathetic states of mind from within, he might easily in this book have overreached himself if he had not maintained a strict consciousness of his own standpoint: with few exceptions Europeans who wander unmoored into the mysterious spaces of Oriental character and soul founder in literary disaster. Yet when he comes to the third and last part of the book "The English," his performance, though superlative at moments, becomes uneven. Possibly, when discussing matter more familiar to him, the strain was relaxed too suddenly. There are passages towards the end where, quite surprisingly, his humour gets out of hand, and notes of facetiousness strike discords in this serious exposition of a profoundly serious theme. And, once again, as in all his previous books, he gives reign to intemperate invective.

The chapter opens with one of his best things:

"From an eminence above the Delhi plain rises a line of sunlit domes and towers, pink and cream against the azure sky—the new capital of India. Few capitals can surpass the magnificence of this architectural monument to the English dominion. Yet on the West coast of India, surrounded by palm trees and lagoons, lingers a ghostly parody of this magnificence, the epitaph of another and earlier European dominion.

There, athwart a road leading from a broken wharf that was once a street, stands another arch, planned for the reception of other Viceroys and upholding, in a creepered niche, the effigy of Vasco da Gama. In the Council House at Panjim may be seen the cracked portraits of these other Viceroys, imperious in ruff, corselet, and peruke of the sixteenth, seventeenth and eighteenth centuries. Up at old Goa, the secular buildings have sunk to mounds beneath the palm trees. But in the series of gigantic churches that still stand; in the twisted Manoeline of St. Francis; in Bom Jesus, where the body of St. Francis Xavier lies embalmed in a tomb supplied by the Grand Duke of Tuscany; in the crypt of St. Monica's, floored with Persian tiles of the seventeenth century that moulder untended and moss-grown in the damp; in the vast aisles of the cathedral, where a few brown-skinned canons in purple and lace still perform their rites to the accompaniment of a mechanical organ; in the bat-stunk dome of St. Cajetan's, a church modelled on St. Peter's . . . may be read the tale of the Portuguese Empire in India, sprung up by decree of Albuqueqrue, and after a century of wealth and might, doomed to fall into a perpetual decline. . . . Misfortune comes to the complacent, brought not by some moral law, but because complacence is the parent of incompetence. The last half of the nineteenth century saw this disease fasten on Englishmen like a cholera."

He contrasts the alarm of English ultra-conservatives and the prophecies of the American press that the English were about to be expelled from Asia, with the enduring position which England has built up in India. This part of the book, an elaboration of his opening chapter, is first rate. He then, unfortunately, breaks into seven pages of invective. It may be remembered that at that time, in 1930, the Viceroy, Lord Irwin, had made a pronounce-ment that our aim in India was to create a dominion on the model existing in the Commonwealth, that this was followed by a Round Table Conference in London at which the Mahatma Ghandi was present, and that this provoked intense opposition which was led by Winston Churchill and publicised by the late Lord Rothermere in the *Daily Mail.* Violent words were used and in this book Robert replied with greater and more insulting violence. The storm has now passed. Mr. Churchill and Mr. Amery, the leaders of the "Anti-Dominion" party, recanted in full in 1941. History may very likely consider that Mr. Churchill's Indian campaign of 1930 was an aberration, and that the other point of view, which Robert voiced so passionately, was the right one. (That is my own opinion.) But temperate statement of his arguments would not only have been far more impressive, and more damning to his opponents, but would have left his book uninjured. As it is, though fair treatment is foregone for a brief seven pages only, this is long enough to give this important and beautiful work the appearance of a political pamphlet. I have mentioned Robert's modesty; here, as on other occasions, he underestimated the enduring value of what he was writing. He was a fighter, and though I would not for the world have had him otherwise, I recognise that it marred him gravely as a writer.

The rest of the book is at once a vivid picture of what Englishmen in India are, and a moving plea for the adoption of English humanity, decency, and tradition in the best sense to the problems of India. The unevenness I mentioned does not seriously disfigure the book: the abiding impression is clear and deep. I say again that this book, even without re-editing, should be read by everyone going for the first time to the East, and a wise administration would see that it was included in official reading; for although it was written in the heat of a past controversy, it remains fresh, true, and profound.

I do not propose to say very much about Robert's next three books, because, although they maintain the standard of writing which he had now achieved, they mark no advance in his development and all had the nature of interludes. They were: *The Appreciation of Architecture*, published in 1932; *First Russia Then Tibet*, 1933; and *Innocence and Design*, 1935.

Of the first of these books, *The Appreciation of Architecture*, I am unable to write, as I have never read it. This is through Robert's wish rather than my own. When we were travelling together in Persia I asked him if he had a copy of this book. He answered rather shortly that he did not wish to be reminded of it, and exacted a promise from me that I would never read it. Some years later I picked up a copy in his rooms. He snatched it from me, saying: "Do you *never* keep promises?" I gather from friends of mine who have read it that it is far from being a contemptible production, indeed that it is an admirable guide to certain principles of architectural æsthetics. I dare say it is a "rehash" of many of the ideas he had already expressed elsewhere, and, in that sense, is not significant. I would like to read it, but I twice gave a promise not to, and though the oath was not very serious it pleases me to keep my word.

First Russia Then Tibet should have been two books. Russia and Tibet are not easily associated in a single study; if he seriously intended to do this, he failed. The centre of gravity is uncertain; there are signs of hurried composition. For all that, this is one of my favourite travel books. It is the most entertaining thing he wrote.

The first part, "Russia," is the most interesting. In the same way as *The Station* was a sketch for *The Byzantine Achievement*, I believe that here, possibly not quite consciously, he was writing the prelude to another greater book on Russia which he never lived to achieve. This, rather than the First Great War, would, I believe, have been the subject of his most lasting work. Russia fascinated him. His early training in Byzantine studies had equipped him with an intense power of observation of this subject, and being entirely free then from Rightist or Leftist prejudice, he saw Russia easily and accurately as a whole. What he left on record in this book is excellent. He showed that he had a feeling for his subject, both in its historical and most modern aspects. I use the word "feeling" to denote nothing superficial. He was one of the few people I have known who always talked sense about Russia; he was neither scared nor deceived.

The second part, "Tibet," is a delicious comedy. It records his journey into Tibet with two friends, Lord Rosse and Lord Faringdon. I cannot resist one quotation:

> "'Oh, you've got a Tibetan hat, have you?' remarked the doctor as we made to depart.
>
> "'Yes,' I answered. 'It's almost saved my life. D'you like it?'
>
> "'Well, I shouldn't wear one myself, you know—not warm enough.' Saying which he assumed a tweed thimble. As the Tibetan hat is probably the warmest hat in the world, he evidently considered me a traitor to the Anglo-Saxon decencies."

This passage gives the spirit of this gay account of a grim land.

The third of these books of interlude is a novel which he and I wrote together, *Innocence and Design*. While we were in Teheran, suffering pettifogging persecution from the Persian officials, he told me one day with a burst of laughter that he was thinking of writing a novel on the subject of Sir Dennison Ross, depicting him as stranded in Persia in the course of a cultural mission. We both laughed ourselves into hysterics over variations which this idea suggested to us in turn. A week or so later Robert was confined to bed and he wrote a couple of chapters. But after this the plan was forgotten. A few months later, Robert was away in Firuzabad (in South Persia) and I was imprisoned in Shiraz. He had left most of his papers and photographs with me, and to while away the tedium of incarceration I added three more chapters to his novel. After his return I was liberated (by a Chief of Police nearly suffocating with giggles), and thereafter we travelled together to North Persia, Trans-Caspia, Afghanistan, India, and so home. During this journey the book became our relaxation. When we reached England we decided it was a masterpiece, and it was published in the next year by Messrs. Macmillan.

I do not pretend to impartial judgment on this novel: I like it very much. It recalls wonderful days to me. It was written for the most part sitting amid saddlebags in the courtyards of caravanserais under magic skies. I own that it was written in intoxicating circumstances, and that the best writing is done without the aid of such stimulants. I suggest, however, that on the credit side one can safely enter that it does present a true picture of Persia under Reza Shah. The latter himself is described accurately. So is General Ayrum, at that time Chief of Police and, as court favourite, discharging the functions of a Grand Vizier. The tragi-comic predicament of Asiatic longing for "progress," and envy of a misunderstood West, is extremely well described. (I can say this, as Robert wrote nearly all the passages on this theme.) On the credit side, I would also add the portrait of Sir Dennison Ross and the Minister Selfridge (a realistic portrait of Mr. Parkes, the Legation chauffeur). On the debit side, I feel obliged to admit that the horseplay, and the extravagant complications of the plot, become out of control, and are occasionally tedious. Some of the jokes are rather foolish. But the main challenge the book incurs is of an odd nature. Robert was absorbed in his study of Persian architecture, and this interest not only intrudes but becomes the main subject of the book. The critical question, therefore, comes ultimately to this: Is it possible to write a farcical novel in a popular style with Ghaznavide architecture (of which most people have never heard) as the hero? I leave the question open.

The tale of Robert's literary career is now nearly done. Let us look back on his achievement.

The first impression is of immense energy, but the second is of frustration. The two are related by the violent nature of his loyalty to things he believed in. The books on Greece, with which he opened his career, illustrate the predicament, and in the *Birth of Western Painting* it is brought to its logical and extravagant conclusion. Under the pressure of his loyalty to a people and a tradition he loved so well, the book, rather than a description of origins, becomes an attack, a condemnation and mockery of Western art. I have suggested that one reason for this aberration was that his capacity for loyalty was in a sense too wide (a most pleasing fault): he extended it to an unsuitable object; his age, his generation. (I mean by that, that time and period cannot be objects of reasoned devotion.) After the production of this last-named book he was considered an extraordinarily brilliant young man, the most distinguished in achievement of that group of clever men produced by mid-twenty Oxford, but not, except by a few, taken more seriously than one should an *enfant terrible* of art and letters, a poker of fun at entrenched authority, a determined wagger of red flags. This was an unjust underestimation. The depth of his talents was disguised by his fireworks.

The *Essay on India* altered the perspective. Here for the first time the long range of his insight and the fine capacity of his mind were made perfectly evident. (At the time this book did not provoke as many people as it should have done to readjust their estimation of him; the attacks on Lord Rothermere and Winston Churchill attracted attention away from the main purpose and argument of the book, and, added to this, the book was published at an unpropitious moment. After the Round Table Conference people grew weary of the subject of India.) He had not yet written a masterpiece. In *The Byzantine Achievement* and the *Essay* he had come near to doing so. In the former he indulged his weaknesses too freely, in the second he was still too much under their spell to shake himself quite free of them. I have tried to indicate by quotation what a remarkable book the *Essay* is. I doubt whether I have succeeded. It is not an easy book to illustrate by selected passages; they give little idea of the sustained excellence of the whole; and the reason for this is to be found, I think, in the fact that quotation accentuates the deficiencies which were still present in his style, deficiencies which are largely responsible for the element of frustration in his early work. I take the opportunity now to consider his style briefly.

The debt which modern English owes to H. W. Fowler can hardly be estimated. If modern English prose is distinguished, it is due, more than to any other single fact, to the influence which his *Modern English Usage*, that wittiest of books of grammar, has exerted on modern writers. But though he was a great reformer, he was also a narrow one. At the time at which he wrote, pompous verbiage was still the chief menace to clear prose expression in the English language, and his life work was devoted to the slaying of that long-lived hydra. (He nearly killed it, but not quite.) He had a mission. All young talents are tempted to make asses of themselves in the purple-light district, and Fowler's discipline put a term to and redeemed many a foolish excursion to those brothels. But there are some rare talents which can only travel easily along a primrose path, and whom ordinary severities can only thwart. Fowler had no message for the few authentic writers of the grand style, of the precious phrase and the emotional passage, and it so happened that Robert was just such a writer, and—a great admirer of Fowler. It may sound absurd, and yet I know for a fact that Robert's aim was to achieve a terse style. He wanted to be another Samuel Butler. He never achieved it, he could not, but he persisted in an endeavour from which his temperament excluded the possibility of success. So to become a

distinguished writer he was condemned to hack out his
own pathway. In all his early books an inclination to
luxurious writing contrasts, without harmony, with
rigorously disciplined expression. The loneliness imposed
on him by his singular temperament preserved many
errors of style. His sense of metaphor remains defective
longer than it need have done; precision becomes harsh-
ness; the short sentences jolt the long.

In consequence of the difficulty which he experienced
in the formation of his style, Robert only wrote super-
latively well when inspired by the majesty of his theme.
The long climax and diminuendo of *The Byzantine
Achievement* is certainly a remarkable and beautiful piece
of writing, and I would say the same of the passage I have
quoted on page 120 from the *Essay on India.* But
such passages are infrequent. I do not wish to exaggerate
his faults of style. He contrived an adequate instrument
for his needs, and if one does not notice the defects on a
first reading, it is because the mass of ideas keeps the
interest diverted from them. But for all that, his style
is not more than adequate to necessity.

As if by magic, all these faults, of style and of composition, fell away from him when he wrote *The Road
to Oxiana,* his last book which I will now consider. It is
nearly ten years since this book was published, and reading
it again now in a critical spirit I have not the slightest
doubt that it can be declared a masterpiece: a little
classic of art history, of humanism and travel. The style
is now at last assured, the luxury and severity are fused
firmly into a satisfying whole; the theme is grasped
confidently, and the result is a unique picture of Persia
in the days of Reza Shah, and an unerring guide to
certain origins, and the character, of Persian architecture.
Nothing Robert wrote was quite perfect. The book has
one very odd fault: a fault of tempo. It is written in the
style of casual jottings during a journey from Venice to
the East, the same style in which the original notes for
the book were made. So conscientiously is it disguised

as a book of hurried entries into a diary that a reader
may easily and pardonably read it too quickly, mistaking
it for an amusing record of an amusing trip, and no more.
It needs to be read slowly. He may have cut down a little
too drastically in his final revision; his modesty, too,
may have played a trick with him, as it did in the *Essay*.
I remember Sir Percy Sykes telling him that he felt he
had underestimated the importance of his achievement,
and Robert seemed impressed when he said this, impressed
with the justice of the criticism rather than with the
compliment. But, even so, it may be argued that "fault"
is not the right word for a gaiety and lightness which
may deceive the inattentive reader as to the gravity of
the main theme.

What is the theme?

It is a quest for the origins of Islamic art.

As I have already told in my study of Bahram Kirmani,
when the mosques of Persia were furtively opened in 1931
a revolution in art criticism was the natural result, for
diverse as have been the influences on the art of Islam,
from Persia, unknown Persia, inspiration has most con-
sistently and wonderfully flowed. With the mosques no
longer closed, a great secret volume of history was at
last open, and Robert was among the first men to report
on the contents. His ideas remain valid. He had achieved
a very finely trained eye.

It would be wrong to say that he presents a thesis: it
would be more sensible to say that he presents the
evidence which exists for a possible thesis. Persia is still
a very puzzling phenomenon to the art historian because
she is a land of frequent renaissances, dependent largely
on foreign influences for her inspirations, yet something
more than a scene of brilliant eclecticism. The evidence is
scattered and mostly destroyed. Theories vary from time
to time as to whether Persia invented such major artistic
features as the dome, the pointed arch, and the glazed
tile; or whether she borrowed these ideas from elsewhere
and improved on them; or whether (noticeably in the case

of domes) she invented them independently of others. One thing only is clear: that the Persian genius has an almost unique ability to adapt new ideas, to produce from conjunctions, new forms. Strangely enough this aspect of the question is most easily followed in the art of ancient pre-Islamic Persia. At that time the most frequent and decisive influences were Western, and in the remains of the Achemenians and Sasanians the influence of Egypt, Babylon, Assyria, Greece and Rome is easily visible. This Western influence diminished after the Mohammedan conquest. Yet from the tenth and eleventh centuries onward Persia continued to be the scene of renaissances, all of different character, all inspired by totally new notions. What new influences wrought upon her ?

Robert does not answer that question. Instead, he indicates the importance of two factors which had long been underestimated: the persistence of the old pre-Islamic Persian traditions and the mediæval influences of Central Asia. The Central Asian influence is difficult to calculate. It is impossible to say with absolute confidence whether the confused story of Islamic art is one of conquerors being charmed into patronage or one of productive rapes. What is certain is that the Persian renaissances follow the great invasions. The Seljuks, the Ghaznavides, the Mongols, and the Timurids, names saturated in blood, are also the names of marvellous artistic epochs.

These facts suggest theories, but Robert resisted the temptation to indulge them, for the story of the last Persian renaissance, that of the Safavides in the sixteenth and seventeenth centuries, though it does not absolutely contradict the notion of Persia as a womb of art dependent on these fearful inseminations, certainly weakens it. The Safavide renaissance was almost entirely a Persian affair. It is the art of the Safavides which has made Persia famous to the world. It gave us Isfahan. The common idea of Persia as a land of cypresses, blue domes, and of languor, by no means an inaccurate idea, owes its existence to a tempting preoccupation with the exquisite epicene art of that flourishing though decadent age.

Robert, in recording these general ideas, which cannot be outlined as briefly as I have done without making some over-simple generalisations, places the high peak of Persian architectural achievement in the time of the Timurids, in the reign of Shah Rukh the son of Tamerlane. While he selects the tomb of King Kabus, built four hundred years before this period, as the greatest surviving monument in middle Asia, he gives his opinion that the most important monument of the greatest age was to be found in the group of buildings, erected in Herat by Gohar Shad (the wife of Shah Rukh), whose ruins still dominate the town. Since their destruction, the mosque adjoining the shrine of the Imam Reza at Meshed is to be considered now as the finest surviving expression of the Timurids. The grandeur and the former completeness of the Herat buildings give them the foremost place. The Mosque of Gohar Shad in Meshed, and the near contemporary mosque of Yazd, though as splendid and exquisite in ornament, are spoilt by the abiding fault of the Persian genius, its superficiality, its fond devotion to façade and scenic effects, at the expense of complete design.

I have given a very rough outline of Robert's theme. It is difficult to say exactly how much he contributed on his own. The time of his visit was a time of exploration, of changing ideas. Arthur Upham Pope was then collecting the material for his monumental survey of Persian art, to which Robert contributed the chapter on Timurid architecture. Herzfeld and Sir Aurel Stein were revolutionising the old simple ideas of early Persian history, Goddard was beginning his great work of restoring and preserving the monuments of Persia. An astonishing part of Robert's achievement was that in this unfamiliar world he showed such an unerring instinct for the true

values of a perplexing scene. His reaction was immediate.
Many people, with more knowledge than he, have been
distracted from appreciating the noble and manly art of
Persia by the foppish loveliness of Isfahan. Even with
the mosques open it was by no means easy to read, more
or less unaided, the record of Persian genius: to perceive
how very much greater art is to be found in the shabby
old congregational mosque of Yazd than in the radiant
gateway of the sacred college of Isfahan. Robert understood without prompting, without help.

As is just discernible in his book, he came near to
engaging in another Byronic struggle: this time between
the art of the Safavides (whose fame has falsified popular
understanding of Persia) and the forgotten glories of
mediæval Persia, Robert, of course, fighting valiantly
against the popular side. I saw this struggle develop and
the threat of war averted. It is an amusing story.

Admirers of Safavide art became known to Robert as
"Omar Khayyám fiends." He often made fearful eructa-
tional noises of disgust over photographs of these glories,
particularly in the presence of admirers. I recall a
morning in Isfahan when he felt reluctantly obliged to
photograph the Safavide buildings; the camera and
tripod were set up in the gardens of an ancient palace,
and I was helping him by sorting out his notes. There
were some notes out of Curzon, and as I read them I
remarked that since his time several more of the palaces,
whose destruction he laments, had disappeared. "Thank
God," groaned Robert from under the hood. I asked him
to take a photograph of the Royal Gate and Balcony (the
Ala Gapu) for me. He did, from behind. Nothing on
earth would induce him then or later to photograph this
amazing piece of decorative building from the front.
The battle was drawing near. Robert was impatient to
lead a charge. Then a curious thing happened. On his
second visit to Isfahan in the Spring of 1934, he, as so
many others have done, fell under the spell of this
irresistible seductress. Without having noted the process

he found himself enchanted. He did not recant, however, until I had taken him inside the mosque of Shaykh Lutf'ullah, the greatest masterpiece of the Safavide period, one of the great masterpieces of the world. After that he had few hard words for the Omar Khayyam fiends, and there were no more eructations. The mosque restored the peace. As a result, his criticism of Safavide art became perfectly balanced in his book.

Those towers about which Robert had asked me when I returned from my first visit to Persia became a prominent part of our lives. They are mediæval tombs, made of brick. I think we visited all those of importance. The largest and most famous one, the eleventh-century tomb of King Kabus on the Turcoman Steppe, Robert believed to be one of the great buildings of the world. Never shall I forget that afternoon twelve years ago when we drove together through a green sea of grassland to this vast tower, standing forth like a lighthouse on its square platform of earth.

Besides the immense advance he made in this book as an art historian and critic, Robert showed the full flowering of other gifts, notably of his humour. Little dialogues occur in nearly all his books. In this one they appear frequently, and better than elsewhere. He had a sometimes uncomfortably sharp power of selection: picking out little absurdities of conversation revealing strange and sometimes rather hideous depths of character.

I will conclude my account of *The Road to Oxiana* by quoting some passages as examples of its many qualities. The following from page 32 illustrates as well as anything he wrote his fully evolved style and gives in the remarkable concluding sentence his own starting point:

"Baalbek is the triumph of stone; of lapidary magnificence on a scale whose language, being still the language of the eye, dwarfs New York into a home of ants. The stone is peach-coloured, and is marked in ruddy gold as the columns of St. Martin-in-the-Fields are marked in soot. It has a marmoreal texture, not transparent, but faintly powdered, like bloom on a plum. Dawn is the time to see it, to look up at the Six Columns, when peach-gold and blue air shine with equal radiance, and even the empty bases that uphold no columns have a living, sun-blest identity against the violent deeps of the firmament. Look up, look up; up this quarried flesh, these thrice enormous shafts, to the broken capitals and the cornice as big as a house, all floating in the blue. Look over the walls, to the green groves of white stemmed poplars; and over them to the distant Lebanon, a shimmer of mauve and blue and gold and rose. Look along the mountains to the void: the desert, that stony, empty sea. Drink the high air. Stroke the stone with your own soft hands. Say goodbye to the West if you own it. And then turn . . . to the East.

"We did, when the ruins closed. It was dusk. Ladies and gentlemen in separate parties were picnicking on a grass meadow, beside a stream. Some sat on chairs by marble fountains, drawing at their hubble-bubbles; others on the grass beneath occasional trees, eating by their own lanterns. The stars came out and the mountain slopes grew black. I felt the peace of Islam. And if I mention this commonplace experience, it is because in Egypt and Turkey that peace is now denied; while in India Islam appears, like everything else, uniquely and exclusively Indian. In a sense it is so; for neither man nor institution can meet that over-powering environment without a change of identity. But I will say this for my own sense: that when travelling in Mahommadan India without previous knowledge of Persia, I compared myself to an Indian observing European classicism, who had started on the shores of the Baltic instead of the Mediterranean."

The following is from an entry made at Baghdad

where our spirits reached an unusual depth of depression (page 36):

"It is little solace to recall that Mesopotamia was *once* so rich, so fertile of art and invention, so hospitable to the Sumerians, the Seleucids, and the Sasanids. The prime fact of Mesopotamian history is that in the XIIIth century Hulagu destroyed the irrigation system; and that from that day to this Mesopotamia has remained a land of mud. . . . It is a mud plain, so flat that a single heron, reposing on one leg beside some rare trickle of water in a ditch, looks as tall as a wireless aerial. From this plain rise villages of mud and cities of mud. The rivers flow with liquid mud. The air is composed of mud refined into a gas. The people are mud-coloured; they wear mud-coloured clothes, and their national hat is nothing more than a formalised mud-pie. Baghdad is the capital one would expect. . . . It lurks in a mud fog; when the temperature drops below 110, the residents complain of the chill and get out their furs. For one thing only is it now famous: a kind of boil which takes nine months to heal and leaves a scar."

Of Sultanya in Azerbaijan (page 50):

"Mile after mile we pursued a straight line between parallel ranges of mountains. The dome of Sultanya loomed over the desert. To reach it we had to break down a whole irrigation system. There we found a different Persia. Though but a few miles off the main road, the modern Pahlevi[1] hat was replaced by the old helm-shaped cap which appears in the reliefs at Persepolis. Most of the villagers spoke Turkish. Securing a bowl of curds and a flap of bread the size of a tent from the tea-house, we entered the mausoleum.

"This remarkable building was finished by the Mongol prince Uljaitu in 1313. An egg-shaped dome

[1] The ski-ing cap referred to in *The Inspiration of a Persian*.

about 100 feet high rests on a tall octagon, and is enclosed by a stockade of eight minarets. . . . The brick is pinkish. But the minarets were originally turquoise, and trefoils of the same colour, outlined in lapis, glitter round the base of the dome. Against the flat desert, pressed about by mud hovels, this gigantic memorial of the Mongol Empire bears witness to that Central Asian virility which produced, under the Seljuks, Mongols and Timurids, the happiest inspirations of Persian architecture. Certainly this is façade-architecture: the prototype of the Taj and a hundred other shrines. But it still breathes power and content, while its offspring achieve only scenic refinement. It has the audacity of true invention; the graces are sacrificed to the idea, and the result, imperfect as it may be, represents the triumph of the idea over technical limitations. Much great architecture is of this kind."

I advised Robert not to set down the name of Reza Shah in his notes in case they were confiscated by the police. He took the advice. Rejecting the well-worn soubriquets of Brown, Jones, or Robinson, already squandered on the Western dictators, he referred to Reza Shah as "Marjoribanks," claiming that the traditional pronunciation of this surname as "Marchbanks" evoked the Emperor's ideals briefly and conclusively. The effect so pleased him that he retained it (with necessary explanations) in the finished product.

On page 54 he describes our arrival at Tabriz:

"At Tabriz the police asked us for five photographs each (they did not get them) and the following information:

Avis

Je soussigné { Robert Byron
              Christopher Sykes

sujet { anglais
        anglais

et exerçant la profession de $\begin{cases} \text{peintre} \\ \text{philosophe} \end{cases}$

declare être arrivé en date du $\begin{cases} 13 \quad \text{Octobre} \\ 13 \quad \text{Octobre} \end{cases}$

accompagné de $\begin{cases} \text{un djinn} \\ \text{un livre par Henry James} \end{cases}$

"The features of Tabriz are a view of plush-coloured mountains, approached by lemon-coloured foothills; a drinkable white wine and a disgusting beer; several miles of superb brick-vaulted bazaars ; and a new municipal garden containing a bronze statue of Marjoribanks in a cloak. There are two monuments: the wreck of the famous blue mosque, veneered in XVth century mosaic; and the Ark, or Citadel, a mountain of small russet bricks laid with consummate art, which looks as if it had once been a mosque, and if so, one of the biggest ever built. Turkish is the only language, except among officials. The merchants were formerly prosperous but have been ruined by Marjoribanks' belief in a planned economy."

The two passages on Baghdad and Tabriz should be read in conjunction with his detailed studies of Meshed and Persepolis. Among the pleasures of the book is the humour of honest anti-climax. I vouch for the truth of the "djinn" and the "livre par Henry James." He suppresses the fact that we celebrated our visit to the Ark by a homosexual waltz at sunset on the fearful summit of it.

On page 77 he describes one of our towers, that of Damghan. My health had broken down as a result of the Abzerbaijan journey, and he is now recording his first journey to Afghanistan, which he did alone, a journey which nearly cost *him* his good health.

"There are two circular grave-towers in (Damghan), which are inscribed and dated as built in the XIth

century, and are constructed of fine but loosely
mortared café-au-lait brick. A ruined mosque, known
as the Tarikh Khaneh or 'History House,' is even
older; its round squat pillars recall an English village
church of the Norman period, and must have inherited
their unexpected Romanesque form from Sasanian
tradition. The whole of Islamic architecture borrowed
from this tradition, once Islam had conquered Persia.
But it is interesting to see the process beginning thus
crudely, before it attains artistic value."

The following description of Afghans in Herat (page
88) recalls to me passages in Mr. E. M. Forster's essays
on Eastern travel.

"The townsmen . . . sport an occasional waistcoat in
the Victorian style, or the high-collared frock-coat of
the Indian Mussulman. But these importations, when
accompanied by a turban as big as a heap of bedclothes,
a cloak of parti-coloured blanket, and loose white peg-
top trousers reaching down to gold-embroidered shoes
of gondola shape, have an exotic gaiety. . . . This is the
Southern fashion, favoured by the Afghans proper.
. . . The most singular costume is that of the neigh-
bouring highlanders, who sail through the streets in
surtouts of stiff white serge, dangling false sleeves,
almost wings, that stretch to the back of the knee and
are pierced in patterns like a stencil. Now and then
a calicó bee-hive with a window at the top flits across
the scene. This is a woman.
"Hawk-eyed and eagle-beaked, the swarthy loose-
knit men swing through the dark bazaar with a devil-
may-care self-confidence. They carry rifles to go shop-
ping as Londoners carry umbrellas. Such ferocity is
partly histrionic. The rifles may not go off. The
physique is not so impressive in the close-fitting
uniform of the soldiers. Even the glare of the eyes is
often due to make-up. But it is a tradition; in a

country where the law runs uncertainly, the appearance of force is half the battle of ordinary business. It may be an inconvenient tradition from the point of view of Government. But at least it has preserved the people's . . . belief in themselves."

A conversation with a familiar type of romantic wandervogel, in this case a Hungarian (page 107):

"' . . . the things I have seen! I cannot tell you of them. I cannot. Aaaaah!' And overcome by his re-collection of them, he buried his head in his hands.

"' Come, Monsieur,' I said, giving him a gentle tap, ' confide in me these terrible experiences. You will feel better for it.'

"' I am not the type, Monsieur, who thinks himself superior to the rest of humanity. Indeed I am no better than others. Perhaps I am worse. But these people, these Afghans, they are not human. They are dogs, brutes. They are lower than the animals.'

"' But why do you say that?'

"' You don't see why, Monsieur? Have you eyes? Look at those men over there. Are they not eating with their hands? With their *hands*? It is frightful. I tell you, Monsieur, in one village I saw a madman and he was naked.'

"He was silent for a little. Then he asked me in a solemn voice: ' You know Stamboul, Monsieur?'

"' Yes.'

"' I lived in Stamboul a year, and I tell you, Monsieur, it is a hell from which there is no way out.'

"' Really. But you, since you are here, did you find a way out?'

"' Thank God, Monsieur, I did.' "

One of the best portraits in the book is of Shir Ahmad Khan, at that time Afghan Ambassador in Tehran, who since then has become Minister for Foreign Affairs in

Kabul; a glorious robust eccentric, of magnificent appearance and with a voice like a hungry lion. Here are some extracts on this subject:

"Shir Ahmad, the Afghan Ambassador, looks like a tiger dressed up as a Jew. I said: ' If your Excellency gives me permission, I am hoping to visit Afghanistan.'

"' Hoping to visit Afghanistan?' (Roaring): ' OF COURSE you will visit Afghanistan.'

". . . he proceeded to Amanullah's tour of Europe. Attended by various noble Italians they were in a box at the Roman opera.

"' Italian lady she sit next to me. She is ' (eyes blazing) ' big lady. Yah! Great? No, fat. She more fat than Madame Egypt (the Egyptian Ministress) and her breast is too big. It fall out of box. Much diamonds and gold on it. I am frightened. I see if it shall be in my face I suffocate.'

"The scene moved to the State Banquet at Buckingham Palace.

"' Prince of Wales he talk to me. I tell him, "Your Royal Highness you are fool!" (Roaring): "You are FOOL!" Prince of Wales he say "Why am I fool?" I tell him "Sir, because you steeple-jump. It is dangerous, dangerous. English peoples not pleased if Your Royal Highness die." King he hear. He tell Queen, "Mary, His Excellency call our son fool." He very angree, very angree. Queen she ask me why her son fool. I say because he steeple-jump. Queen say to me, "Your Excellency, Your Excellency, you are right, you are right." Queen thank me. King thank me.' "

There are many even funnier examples of this astonishing man's conversation recorded at length.

After his first visit to Herat in the winter of 1933 he came back to Tehran, as the passes to Turkestan were blocked by snow, and his health was worrying him. He contracted some kind of internal poisoning from which

I do not think he ever entirely recovered. In the spring of 1934 we went together to South Persia. In the following description of Shapur, which is near Kazerun, on the Shiraz-Gulf road, he sums up the monumental art of the Sasanians (the immediate pre-Islamic dynasty) with enjoyable accuracy (page 176).

"The place was named after its founder, Shapur I., whose relations with the gods, numerous victories, and capture of the Roman Emperor Valerian are depicted on the walls of a miniature gorge. As documents, these reliefs give a detailed picture of Sasanian fashions in harness, hats, trousers, shoes and weapons. As monuments, they are an interesting survival of that uncouth impulse which prompted the early monarchies of Egypt, Mesopotamia, and Iran to hew themselves immortality out of the living rock. As works of art, they have borrowed from Rome, possibly through Roman prisoners, and mask their barbarous ostentation under a veneer of Mediterranean stateliness and opulence. Those who admire force without art, and form without mind, find them lovely."

One of the best passages in the book occurs ten pages later in his account of Persepolis. It is a long sustained passage, not quotable except in entirety. Few ruins are surrounded by such romantic glamour as these and yet few travellers have failed to see through the glamour, to what Robert calls the "disconcerting void" beyond it. It represents Persian art with all the eclecticism, refinement, precision, and opulence of its subsequent achievements, but with hardly a trace of the inspiration which was to make Persia fabulous for beauty.

Robert's essay on Persepolis is a masterly analysis of what many had detected before him. There was nothing for him to add.

After Persepolis he went back to Isfahan. I like this dialogue which occurred at a tea party given by the Governor:

" I sat between the English Bishop and a Kajar prince.
"' Why are you out here?' asked the bishop angrily.
"' Travelling.'
"' What in?' "

Isfahan was followed by our journey to the Turkoman
Steppe and the tower of King Kabus, and thence to
Meshed. By the time we reached the latter we had both
been imprisoned (myself for the second time), as Englishmen frequently were in those days. We were the material
of Persian holidays, as I have indicated in my account of
our frequent companion Bahram. On arrival at Meshed
we decided to risk a further scandal and enter the shrine,
which was one of the few mosques still closed to unbelievers. Robert tells of the comedy of this adventure,
of our nocturnal prowlings in the sacred buildings. He
only once braved the terrors of the place in daylight. My
height made me unhappily conspicuous, so in order not
to endanger his chances on this occasion I remained as
a reinforcement outside in case of trouble. His disguise
was remarkable, but he could not stay in the great
courtyard of Gohar Shad for more than ten minutes.

During the war I visited this shrine at leisure. I had
Robert's book with me. I am still astonished at the fullness and accuracy of his description of this immense area
of Timurid tile-work.

After Meshed we travelled through Afghanistan and
Turkestan. I cannot resist quoting from a joint production which he includes in his book and which still
makes me laugh aloud to remember. Arrived at Mazar-i-
Sharif in Turkestan, we were both seized with a
desire to visit the Oxus, which was only forty miles away.
But there were difficulties. The region was in a state of
disturbance and permission for this journey was not to
be obtained by the ordinary means. We had made friends,
however, with an Indian doctor, one of the most delightful men I have ever met, Abulmajid Khan, and
he suggested Machiavellian tactics to us—namely, that

we should write to the Minister of State, Muhammad Gul, asking for the permission, but in a form of English which no one but our friend could possibly translate. He would then be summoned, and he would take the occasion, he promised us, to put in a good word. The result ran as follows:

"YOUR EXCELLENCY,

"Knowing from personal experience that Your Excellency's day is already too short for the public welfare, it is with signal reluctance that ... we venture to lay before Your Excellency a trifling personal request.

"In undertaking the journey from England to Afghan Turkestan, whose tedium and exertions have already been thrice repaid by the spectacle of your Excellency's beneficent administration, our capital object was to behold, with our own eyes, the waters of the Amu Darya, famed in history and romance as the river Oxus, and the theme of a celebrated English poem from the sacred pen of Matthew Arnold. We now find ourselves, after seven months' anticipation, within forty miles of its banks.

"Understanding from the secretary of His Ex-cellency the Mudir-i-Kharija that an extraordinary permission is necessary to visit the River we request this permission for ourselves, confident that Your Excellency will not be deluded into imputing a political motive to what is but the natural curiosity of an educated man. ...

"There are indeed some countries where the Light of Progress has yet to pierce the night of mediæval barbarism. ... But we consoled ourselves, during our stay in Persia, by the consideration that we should soon be in Afghanistan, and should thus escape from a parcel of vain and hysterical women to an erect and manly people, immune from ridiculous alarms, and happy to accord that liberty to strangers which they justly demand for themselves.

"Were we right? . . . The answer lies with Your Excellency. Certainly we shall tell of the hotel in Mazar-i-Sharif equipped with every comfort known to the great capitals of the West; of a city in course of reconstruction on lines that London itself might envy; of bazaars stocked with all the amenities of civilisation. But are we then to add that though Your Excellency's capital holds everything to delight the visitor, nevertheless the chief, the unique attraction of the district is denied him? Etc., etc."

I cannot now remember which of us wrote which sentences of this grotesque document. I only lay claim to having added the adjective to Matthew Arnold's pen. The remark about the hotel, in which, hardened as we were by the life of caravanserais, we suffered agonies of discomfort, was, I think, ill-judged. Muhammad Gul is a far-sighted man, and unless I am mistaken, he knew enough about Europe to see through us on this occasion. At all events the permission was refused and we only saw the Oxus at a great distance.

Here is a description of Oxiana, of the country between Andkhoi and Balkh, which I would select as the finest example of Robert's later writing:

"After Akcha the colour of the landscape changed from lead to aluminium, pallid and deathly, as if the sun had been sucking away its gaiety for thousands and thousands of years; for this was now the plain of Balkh, and Balkh they say is the oldest city in the world. The clumps of green trees, the fountain-shaped tufts of coarse cutting grass, stood out almost black against this mortal tint. Sometimes we saw a field of barley; it was ripe, and Turcomans, naked to the waist, were reaping it with sickles. But it was not brown or gold, telling of Ceres and plenty. It seemed to have turned prematurely white, like the hair of a madman—to have lost its nourishment. And from these acrid cerements, first on the north and then on the south of the road, rose the worn grey-white shapes of a bygone architecture, mounds, furrowed and bleached by the rain and sun, wearier than any human works I ever saw: a twisted pyramid, a tapering platform, a clump of battlements, a crouching beast, all familiars of the Bactrian Greeks, and of Marco Polo after them. They ought to have vanished. But the very impact of the sun, calling out the obstinacy of their ashen clay, has conserved some inextinguishable spark of form, a spark such as a Roman earthwork or a grass-grown barrow has not, which still flickers on against a world brighter than itself, tired as only a suicide frustrated can be tired.

"Yet by degrees the country became greener, pasture covered the adamant earth, trees multiplied, and suddenly a line of bony dilapidated walls jumped out of the ground and occupied the horizon. Passing inside them we found ourselves amid a vast metropolis of ruins stretching away to the north; while on the south of the road, the shining greens of mulberries, poplars, and stately isolated planes were balm to eyes bruised by the monstrous antiquity of the preceding landscape. We stood in Balkh herself, the Mother of Cities.

"Our guard surveying the ruins, which were mostly left in this state by Jenghis Khan, remarked: It was a beautiful place till the Bolsheviks destroyed it eight years ago."

There are many excellent touches of description, criticism, and humour which I could quote further to illustrate the quality of this book, but though it was better than any of his other productions, I find difficulty in illustration, not for the reasons I mentioned in the case of the *Essay*, but because the picture is painted in wide sweeps. So I will add no more. It was sometimes said, by old stagers, that Robert wrote about the East without long experience. Would that more people with such talents did so! Morier was never an old stager; Lord Curzon spent less than a year in Persia; Richards, the only modern artist to depict Persia intelligibly, spent only a few months on his travels. Nay, the difficult thing is to find a man who has spent a lifetime in Eastern lands who can produce something one half as good as did these men.

When the book appeared in 1937 it enjoyed a *succés d'estime*. Most critics reviewed it as a collection of amusing jottings, and to my deep regret I must own that I did not perceive till much later what a remarkable book my friend had written. I think I am right in saying that G. M. Young was the only critic to appraise it at its worth. This failure of the moment was due, I think (certainly in my own case), to the queer fault I mentioned earlier: the fault of tempo. One cannot, in literature, as in music, mark the speed at which passages should be read; a writer cannot put "adagio," "lento ma con brio," or "presto," in front of different passages. If the speed of a passage is not implicit in the style, it must be counted as error. Well, that is the error of the book; but a reader who reads slowly, who is not deceived by the diary form of the book, will find an astonishing document of what I may term the first modernity-mad age as it was terribly reflected in Asia from Europe, and also an absolutely reliable guide to the puzzling question of Islamic art and its origins. He will also be entertained by a good story well told.

With this book, published three years before the end of his life, Robert's literary career may be said to have closed. He wrote one or two small things in the few years of peace which remained, but nothing which may be considered as a continuation or addition to his writing life. A change came over him which I hope to indicate in the last part of this essay in which I shall attempt a description of him as a man.

As in his books, the first impression which this remarkable man made in life was of energy—a stormy, almost uncontrollable energy. How well I remember my first sight of him on our journey together to Persia! We had arranged to meet in Venice at the house of our friends Sir Robert and Lady Diana Abdy, but I found on arrival there that he had already left Venice for Cyprus. I followed him by the next boat, and spent a day scouring the island in vain for a trace of him. I grew anxious. Twilight was falling rapidly and the boat due to sail in a few minutes, when to my relief I saw a round figure dressed in jodhpurs and a tweed jacket, and with a cigarette dangling from his lower lip, fairly charging along the jetty to a sound of clattering cameras, pencil-cases and folios which hung about him. A gigantic negro followed at a half-run with his bags. I watched from the deck. Arrived at the boat he showed his ticket, returned it to his pocket, and then made a sort of dive at the officials, as it were, swam through them on a breast-stroke, and mounted the gangway. "Hallo, I'm late," he said, and added as the official bellowings from below reached us: "I had all my papers stamped this morning to save time. It never does to argue with Customs people." I went down the gangway, and not for the last time in my life with him, made peace with an angered crowd.

There then followed our gradual progress to Persia. We went first to Jerusalem, and thence to Damascus, Baalbek and Beirut, where we waited for the rest of our party. We were supposed to meet some explorers who were allegedly traversing Asia on charcoal-driven cars. They had engaged to transport us to Persia from Syria, but their expedition was a long time in coming. I think they found that their cars did not go very well on charcoal. After some time we decided to forget about them and crossed over from Damascus to Baghdad. A

few days later we were in Tehran installed in the Pension
Coq d'Or, and a week or so after this we were in Azerbaijan visiting the first of our brick towers at Maragha.
From this town we rode on horseback across little known
country (from the architectural point of view) to the
Kazvin highway on the other side of the province, a ride
which took us about six days. By the time we reached
Tehran one midnight we knew each other better than
people usually do.

Robert's experience of the East had been gained in
India. It is a curious fact, which has often been noted by
Orientalists, that Persia and India are absolute antitheses.
India has an eternal problem of over-population, Persia is
a land of empty spaces and tiny oases. Indian ideas are
coloured by notions of caste; Persia has the most
egalitarian society in the world. India is a sub-continent
of Asia; Persia is like a piece of Europe which has fallen
into Islam. Very few Indians indeed learn to speak
Persian correctly. Indians get the wrong end of every
Persian verbal stick. Even Europeans who learn their
Persian in Calcutta talk with a kind of twist in the
language for ever after, no matter how hard they may
study later in Persia. The Persian word for "devil"
figures in Urdu as the name of God. An extraordinary
division, never explained fully, separates Persians from
Indians, both in character and temperament. An Englishman of England finds no great difficulty in understanding
what is afoot and what he should do in Persia. An
Englishman with experience of India, trained to deal
with far more complicated and baffling emergencies,
rarely succeeds in not putting his foot in it if called on
to deal with affairs in Persia. He finds a situation which
taxes his pliancy of character to the limit.

It interested me to follow Robert in this dilemma. I
could see that at first he was puzzled, that he felt
in an uncomfortably new yet familiar atmosphere.
I saw also the intense mental effort which it cost him to
forget a lot he had learned in India and replace it by

understanding of this easy-going yet severely formal society into which he had strayed; and it seemed to me that, because the mental effort needed was so thorough, the result was so successful. In innumerable small observations in his book Robert showed that he understood the Persian world as very few have done. This understanding first came about on our journey in Azerbaijan, and I remember the extremely odd incident, a little episode of purest farce, which marked the moment when Robert had succeeded in readjusting his mental gears.

We were being entertained to supper by a headman in an Azerbaijan village. At the end of the meal there was the usual chorus of regurgitation in which I joined freely.

"Must you make that disgusting noise?" asked Robert a little primly.

"It's customary. Didn't you find the same thing in India?"

"In India," replied Robert, looking down his nose, "English people don't ape native customs."

"Nor should they here. I like belching. They like me to belch. I belch."

"I see." He looked at our hosts pensively.

The next night we stayed with another headman, who organised another carouse. At the end of it we were all sitting round the fire on the floor, and I was making our side of the conversation, when suddenly from silent Robert there came a noise like an earthquake or of a hurricane mixed with a cannonade. Familiar as our hosts must have been with the whole scale of soniferous digestion this noise shook them considerably. It was from the time of this incident that I noticed that Robert was inwardly at peace in Persia.

Although he was gifted with unusual vision, Robert, in spite of the breadth of view he attained, worked on the dark-lantern system. When he studied, and his life was spent in study, he collected the whole light of his mind in a single direction. I think he lived a life of extraordinary mental strain, not so much during the periods when he was searching for information as when he was assembling it, placing it in juxtaposition with other prizes, and attempting the formation of that complete view of life and the world which was his great and consistent aim. Here in Persia, for example, by a mighty effort, he placed himself in a mental state where he could allow his imagination to wander amid Persian sympathies. He was happy in Persia. He understood the people, their history, and artistic expression. But the effort of writing *The Road to Oxiana*, an effort which cost him three years of hard work, was not so much in writing the first draft here in Persia, but afterwards, when he set his observations amid the experiences of his full life.

The natural state of his mind, to correct which cost him often such toil, might perhaps be compared more happily to a lighthouse than to a dark lantern. Many beams struck out far in many directions, but between the beams was darkness. He was a curious case of vision and blindness together, of natural light and darkness. The light was never weak, the darkness often profound. Let me illustrate this.

Certain ordinarily accepted ideas baffled him totally. It was to him partly a mystery, partly a horrible proof of the vileness of normal taste, that the Dutch and Flemish masters are considered with universal respect. That Rembrandt was thought to be one of the great artists of the world was a fact which administered to him an unremitting sense of disgust. (He believed that Breughel was the solitary great artist produced by the Low Countries). I narrowly missed a physical assault when·I told him during our ride that I had an enormous admiration for Rembrandt. I put it to him (when he was calm once more) that Rembrandt was like Wagner, an immortal who had perhaps taken the wrong path, but surely legitimately enjoyable to mortals provided they used discrimination. I said: "You don't play Mozart and Wagner at the same concert; why not forget El Greco when you look at Rembrandt?" Robert could hardly contain himself. "You mean," he half-shouted, half-snorted, "you don't play rag-time!"

His dislike of the Dutch painters (they are not once mentioned in the *Birth of Western Painting*!) was in tune with much modern predilection, but he sometimes entered lonelier fields of preference. I was astonished to learn from him as we rode our weary horses through those interminable golden plains of Azerbaijan, that among the objects wholly obscured from his appreciation were the works of William Shakespeare, though in this, as opposed to the question of Rembrandt, he admitted to an uneasy feeling that he might be wrong. He had tried, he said, very hard, to extract some glimmer of sense or beauty from the works of the greatest of poets, but he had found nothing but verbosity and bosh. "Would you kindly explain to me," he asked with dangerous coolness, "why, for example, King Lear is thought to be so *awfully* good?" I explained to the best of my ability. "They all say that," he sighed, "and just to make sure, I went to see Gielgud acting it the other day. Perhaps I didn't understand a word. Perhaps. But it seemed to me as though I understood only too plainly. Good God! What rot!" I told him that Tolstoy had found himself in the same predicament: alone in a Shakesprolatrous world, either insane or unique in his sanity. I found a copy of Tolstoy's famous denunciation later and gave it to him. I shall never forget the joy with which he read it. He told me he agreed with every word.

I have recorded in another book the most amusing manifestation I remember of this astonishing prejudice of his, but I think I may repeat it now. When Robert and I were in Russia, I was having a Russian lesson from a lady in the service of Intourist (and also of the G.P.U., as she told me), and while I was struggling with the language in one corner of the room, Robert was working at his papers in the other corner. My instructress was a

woman of such engaging intelligence, and I find the
Russian language so intolerably difficult, that I en-
couraged frequent recuperation periods in English, and
it was during one of these that our Russian friend told
me that she was an enthusiastic student of Shakespeare.
She was not a very orthodox one, however. She had
discovered early in her researches, she told me, that there
could be no question of William Shakespeare being the
author of the plays attributed to him; it was out of the
question. Bacon? No, the evidence was too slight. She
had toyed with the WHs for a while until she had been
led to a conclusive and irrefutable discovery: that the
author was Shakespeare's contemporary, the Earl of
Rutland. She was a Rutlandian. She invited comment.
Heaven knows where she had got all this stuff from!

"Well," I said, "I never really understand the original
objection. Why is poor Shakespeare disqualified before
any one else?"

"Oh, really! That is quite obvious. He was a Stratford
grocer, and these plays are the works of a great man of
the world."

Robert joined in at this moment. "That's exactly
where all you Baconians and people go wrong. If these
plays were known as Bacon's plays, or Lord Rutland's
plays, I should object most vigorously that they must
have been written by someone else: in fact, by a grocer."
He settled down to his papers once more. "They are
exactly the sort of plays," he murmured, "that I would
expect a grocer to write."

Northern European art, and Shakespeare, were among
several matters shrouded for him in this strange darkness,
but the greatest surprise for me was to discover that one
of the blind spots of his bright vision covered the subject
of himself. He had extraordinarily misleading ideas as
to what manner of man he was. He was a violent tem-
pestuous man, of such burning convictions about so
many things that he often greatly scared people who
did not know him, and did not know how much good

nature went along with his fighting spirit, and that there was another gentle sweet side to his nature. But Robert's own opinion was that he figured in the world as a timid little fellow, an unnoticed and courtly nonentity. Referring to the colour of his eyes, he used to describe himself as a "green mouse." I can think of no one I have ever met whom I would so reluctantly include in the category of green mice, yet this was Robert's considered view of himself. It was only one of his misinterpretations of his character.

For sheer fun and humour Robert was an unrivalled companion—often he kept me in fits of laughter for hours on end. I still remember his description of an Oxford group meeting as the highest peak of imitative farce I have ever witnessed. Yet he sometimes, I do not say often, found himself wondering whether he was not, in fact, stolidly humourless. He had a very unusual sense of humour, and this fact, I think, made him sometimes suppose he was deficient in that quality. He could not follow conventional humour: smoking-room stories, jokes about Aberdonians, the usual stock-in-trade of barmen, left him perplexed and bewildered, and that odd streak of modesty which shot through his character occasionally inclined him to suppose that had he been a person of brighter, quicker mind he would have found these things exceedingly diverting.

The humour of his talk was almost exactly the same as is found in his books. I used to enjoy it best, I think, when indignation excited angry derision, and the adjectives would come bursting out, one slowly after the other, ponderously; and then the style would change in a flash, and the victim was ridiculed in high mock-mincing tones. He had as well a peculiar style of humorous drawing which he unfortunately neglected. There is an excellent youthful effort of his, depicting the 4th June at Eton, which shows more promise than he ever had time to fulfil. One of the best drawings he ever did was done during our journey through Azerbaijan—a grotesque portrait of

myself shaving, entitled "Crag's Toilet." It shows that,
given time to mature this talent, he might have become
a skilled comic draughtsman, somewhat in the style of
Sir Max Beerbohm. His preoccupations robbed the
world of a caricaturist; but they gave us a unique writer
who did more, I believe, to educate the world than the
world is likely to give him credit for.

These odd unpredictable failures, these brief but total
suspensions of his vision, showed, I think, two main
points of his character; first at what cost, because with
what unusual concentration, he directed the beams of
his insight on the objects of his particular studies; and
secondly, of what an outward-facing kind he was. The
idea of Robert as an extrovert is not easily acquired from
his books with their frequent flashes of introspective
brilliance, yet such he was in the essence of his character.
It is to be noticed in his books that when he discusses
himself he does so with detachment, and because he
conceives it as necessary to the argument to examine
intimate processes. Though he was a child of his age,
particularly in the sense that he loved and believed in it,
he was a total stranger to the intense cult of self-
examination which the example of psycho-analysis
excited so many contemporary writers to follow.

These considerations lead to a generalisation which,
I think, is as valid as such pronouncements can be: that
he was a man of extremes, that his talents were wrought
to extreme heights of intensity, but that this very
intensity left gaps of exhaustion in him. His gaunt
conviction, which I cannot believe was a true one, that
all realistic and representational art was fallacious,
occurred as a desert, to offset the intense and marvellous
understanding he had of the Byzantines and of El Greco,
the fertile lands we may call them, the luxurious gardens
of his mind.

This character of extremes, of contrast, was very
discernible in the functioning of that energy which I
have selected as his most prominent feature. Whenever

I think of Russia, Persia, or the East, I see Robert with his rapid footsteps, hunched shoulders, load of cameras and drawing gear, and a cigarette in his mouth, which he never seemed to have time to remove for a moment, and whose continual presence often made him breathe with a sort of subdued roar. He always seemed to be dashing from minaret to mosque, or cathedral to new architectural view. Idleness was not a temptation he resisted, but a state which he loathed. And yet this violent energy would come to sudden stops. He used often, sometimes daily, to tax his strength so highly that it suddenly went out, like a guttered candle. People who met him at dinner sometimes formed odd opinions of him. I have seen him sit down at a dinner-party, and before five minutes drop off into a profound sleep, from which repeated shakings could not arouse him. A comfortable chair in a comfortable room after a hard day was fatal: a snore would echo through the room and Robert was "out" for the evening. A delightful Englishwoman who used often to entertain us in Tehran once asked me what my friend was like.

"But you've seen him every day for a month," I said.

"That's true," she said, "but I've only seen him asleep."

I could believe that was true.

These spells of reactionary lethargy were not of long duration, indeed they were sometimes uncomfortably short. I have known evenings when he would wake up towards eleven, when everyone else was ready for sleep, and insist on a few hours' fun.

With this unremitting energy, punctuated by fits of sleepy reaction, there went a corresponding hardness of body which he certainly overstrained on these Eastern journeys of ours. Often I became an unwilling mixture of nurse and governess to him, the sort of nurse or governess, I would add, who gives notice in floods of tears. There was a demon of energy in him which prevented him "playing steady." Once, I remember, we

came to a high range, to overcome which it was necessary
to dismount and plod on foot. The altitude was disagreeably high. Robert set off with his usual short
vigorous steps. "For Heaven's sake," I cried, "don't try
to climb a hill that way. Walk slowly. Reserve your
strength." He turned on me furiously. "Do you mind,"
he said, "if I climb this hill" (with some adjectives) "in
my own way?" He was coughing and blowing at the
top. "Scout-master!" he managed to splutter at me when
I arrived with the caravan.

He had the greatest contempt for showy travellers
who "rough it" for the sake of "roughing it." He liked
to travel with the maximum of reasonable or obtainable
comfort. In this we were agreed, but I remember among
those frequent contrasts which were bound up with his
character an occasion which was a precise antithesis of
the episode of the mountain range. It occurred long
after our Azerbaijan journey on the road to Turkestan
in East Persia. We had stopped through exhaustion on a
stormy night at a weird primitive little coffee-house miles
away from anywhere. Robert settled himself in an upper
room and I slept near the fire below. At about five in the
morning a car arrived, and the driver told me that a river
a few miles ahead was rising. In half an hour it might
be impossible to cross. I dashed up to Robert's room
and told him we must be off straight away. He agreed.
"But first," he said, "I must have some morning tea."

A few minutes later I came back to tell him to get up.
There was no tea. Time was short.

"I need tea," said Robert, "before I get up."

"But there isn't any. Come on, quickly."

"There's always tea in Persia."

"Yes, but not here. For God's sake get up."

"Of course," he said, "but first I must have a little
tea. I need it."

With a howl of exasperation I went downstairs. We
could have some tea in twenty minutes perhaps. I went
back to Robert.

"We're loading the car," I said. "Tea takes too long. Do get up."

"I will when the tea comes."

I kicked an empty petrol tin across the mud floor.

"For Christ's sake," I screamed, "get up!"

"One of my principles," said Robert, with conviction, "is to have tea first."

We loaded the luggage, including Robert's bags, his camera, even some of his bedclothes. And then when everything was ready, except for Robert sitting in his camp-bed in his pyjamas, a man arrived bearing tea. He drank it and we went off, just in time, for the water was indeed rising rapidly.

In describing these contrasts, of vision and blind spots, of energy and dead reaction, of hardness and narrow principles of comfort, I may give the impression that Robert was an impossible companion in travel. I want to give the opposite impression. He was an adorable companion. These absurd comedies were all part of the fun of his companionship. When I traversed our way again in the war, how often I thought with renewed pain of the yawning gap which his death had left behind, how often I remembered, with tears, the ludicrous disputes or the sudden revelations of his vision which the sight of some forgotten coffee-house or caravanserai on the road-side brought back again to my mind. He was a matchless creature.

The journey which we did together in Persia and Afghanistan is better recorded in Robert's book, *The Road to Oxiana*, than I can hope to do here. Let me leave it there, and not try to do again what he did so superbly. It used to fascinate me to watch the book taking its first rough shape on the road. It grew abundantly and profusely, and was then submitted to drastic pruning operations which occasionally, in my opinion, were somewhat too drastic. He was less frightened of his besetting faults of pugnacity and invective than of his occasional over-extravagance of phrase, his liability to indiscretions of impassioned writing. It was fear of this, I suppose, which led him to suppress an extraordinary circumstance in his narrative. When we arrived at Balkh, in Turkestan, that city turned into ruins by the Mongols and reputed to be the most ancient in the world, the moment of our arrival at the shrine in the centre coincided with the bursting of a terrific rainless thunderstorm. A more dramatic first sight of a historic monument could hardly be imagined; the bright blue of the shattered dome lit by flashes and standing out from the deep blue of the thunder-clouds. Yet of this overpowering incident there is no mention in the book.

Only once did Robert misrepresent the facts of our adventure, and I feel that I will not be accused of malice if I tell the true story now. On page 300 he describes a party which the Russian Consul in Turkestan gave for us. He mentions that he fell into a torpor. Any one who has enjoyed Russian hospitality knows the extremes to which it is liable to be taken: the innumerable toasts, the obligation to drain every glass. I was more fortunate than Robert on this occasion, as, sitting by the window, I was able to pour as much liquor clandestinely into the garden as openly down my throat. Without this advantage, Robert not only fell into a torpor, but knocked out the Consular doctor, who rather unnecessarily awoke Robert from his sleep in the garden, whither he had been carried, in order to apply artificial respiration. Robert's remorse in the morning was extreme, but so little could he resist the comedy of the situation that he felt he must somehow record it in his book. He had no objection, he said, to owning to his excesses, but from the artistic point of view he thought that a recital of what had occurred would detract from the seriousness which a first person singular must assume in the kind of book he was planning. He then made the utterly preposterous suggestion that our rôles should be reversed, that I should be represented as passing through *his* adventures, while he would assume the slightly more innocuous part which

I had played in this feast. When I did not agree, he paid the only compliment, an oblique one, which I ever heard him offer to the Roman Catholic Church.

"I'm disappointed," he said, "to find you're so damned Protestant. You wrecked the whole party last night by being so damned Protestant."

A few weeks after these hectic days in Turkestan we left Asia together from Bombay. As the boat sailed, we dramatically dropped our topees into the sea to the perplexity of some of the passengers. It was a moment which required some sort of symbolical identification. It was the end of the last carefree period of our lives. It was the end of a year of life lived as fully and intensely as it is possible to live it, and I would not be surprised if Robert's record of it gives him a permanent place in Oriental and humanist studies. His friend, G. M. Young, first detected that he was that now rare specimen, a humanist. Let us hope he was not the last.

In the winter of 1934 we saw a lot of each other, as we were engaged in polishing and tidying our untidy novel. I used to go down and stay with him and his family in Savernake Forest. I saw the extraordinary manner in which he worked, using a typewriter as freely as a pen, with the cigarette never out of his mouth, and the wireless bellowing classical music at him. Few other people could have written a word under such circumstances.

In September of the next year we went together as delegates to a Conference and Exhibition of Persian Art in Leningrad and Moscow. We stayed on for a month after the Conference had closed, and then in Moscow we parted. I went back to England. He went to China. I did not see him till his return more than a year later. From then till the end of his life we saw each other frequently. A new, the last, phase of his life opened.

The story of Robert's life is not one of heroism in the

ordinary sense of that word. It is a story rather of valiantly obstinate sincerity. The last phase was like that ancient form in music, the Passacaglia, a form in which one theme is repeated throughout, and while the secondary themes are piled high in elaborate construction, the basic theme is never varied or silent. For Robert the basic theme was our duty to defend our civilisation.

In the early autumn of 1936 we had a joyous reunion when he arrived to spend a week with my family in the East Riding of Yorkshire. Since we had last met, he had travelled across Russia and spent a year in China and the United States; he had also finished writing his book which was shortly to be published. We spent a happy week together, riding, hunting, laughing, and talking. Robert was not yet the violent prophet of approaching doom which he was to become before the storm broke, but though he was little changed, though the fun and merriment were as strong and prominent as ever, the seriousness of a deep preoccupation was easily discerned. It was as though the basic theme was being announced calmly on the strings.

He remained a fighter to the end, but he had acquired the calm of conscious strength. Many prejudices were falling away, many of the bees which had buzzed so furiously in his bonnet had flown away through discovered outlets. There was now, for example, no trace of the anti-classical bee; on the contrary, he had become a champion of our English classical heritage, and had already, with his friend Lord Rosse, begun the formation of the Georgian Group, whose aim was to preserve the eighteenth-century architecture of England against English philistinism. The "patriotism in our age" had formed into a finer and more rational loyalty; into a patriotism in our civilisation. He had seen a large part of the world by now, he had turned the beams of the dark lantern on to many different objects, and he was acquiring greater facility in the correlation of experience. I think he had made his mind more flexible by writing about

Persian architecture in the very different environment of China. His life began to reveal itself to him as a great experiment in cross reference. He had studied Europe from Greece, England from India, Byzantium from Russia, Persia from China, and Europe again from the United States. He had learned toleration. This appeared immediately in one fact. In all his books (with the exception of his last) expressions of hostility to the United States appear. They have figured in the quotations I have made, not because I have wished to illustrate this point, but because of the frequency with which these expressions occur. He now recognised that he had made a considerable error on a great subject through impatience over small things, and from being an enemy he became an enthusiastic admirer. He loved and deeply respected America. He had achieved a Weltanschauung, using that term literally. He was not so very far from the realisation of his vast youthful ambition.

His sense of being a European was as strong as ever but modified. In the past he had tended at times to think of Europe as the solitary scene of civilisation in a world devoted elsewhere to outrageous paganisms. China and the United States had broadened this view. He now saw Europe as one of the essentials of civilisation as we know it but not as the sole repository. If Europe should fail, or break asunder, civilisation would go on, but elsewhere and impoverished for long, perhaps for ever, just as in his belief the civilisation of Western Europe had been permanently impoverished by the destruction of its Byzantine predecessor. For these reasons, and on these conditions, it was now the duty of every European to save Europe. One thing perplexed him: that so few people felt as he did. "It's a queer unexpected sensation," he told me one day in Yorkshire, "to find that the only person talking sense in this country is Winston Churchill."

He felt that History might be repeating itself. It was as though we were again in the year 1453. The Turkish hosts had arrived on the Asiatic shore of the Bosphorus, and the men of The City did not seem to be particularly interested.

During the first three months after his return to England Robert was occupied with seeing his book through the press and planning his future. Several offers were open to him. He wanted work which left him sufficient freedom to pursue his chosen interests, and which would allow him to conduct his newly conceived political campaign, which he saw, with increasing clarity, as a duty thrust upon him. Once more he found himself with a task neglected by others; once more, and now most strongly, his reaction to this discovery was not egotistical but indignant. Then while he was endeavouring to make up his mind, he was invited by the newly formed British Council to lecture abroad, in Belgium, Holland, Poland, and the Baltic states, on English life and civilisation. He was away during February and March of 1937, and he returned with his convictions deepened. In the course of this journey he had made his first journey to Nazi Germany.

There is a distinct difference between enthusiastic conviction and fanaticism. Robert had the first, he never allowed his mind to become tainted with the second. He understood the psychology and the meaning of Nazi-ism as few people have done, as few do even now. He loathed Nazi-ism with an instinctive and reasoned abhorrence. Yet this depth of feeling and this precise intellectual disapproval did not smother sympathy. The truth was that he was utterly fascinated by the spectacle of German degeneracy. I think I understand the position of his mind in this matter. For many years he had entertained ambitions, how wisely it would be hard to say, of writing a great work of fiction. He had for long been training his mind to observe his fellow-men with a novelist's eye. Suddenly in Germany he found an abundance of literary raw material the study of which gave him extreme æsthetic excitement, and this experience introduced an element of personal sympathy into his criticism—the sympathy of understanding. I want to make this point very clear. Robert had no delusions about Nazi-ism, his detestation and disapproval were extreme, but he understood the process whereby Germans relapsed into this form of barbarism so well that he never saw it in superstitious terms, but in plain human terms. He never gave way to a feeling of mad general hatred for the Germans.

I saw him very soon after his return in the spring of 1937. He told me of the incident which had forced on his mind anew the enormity of Europe's danger; the Jewish Exhibition, he said, an elaborate anti-Semitic display disguised as anthropology, had at last shown him, beyond all disguise, the depth of Nazi vileness. He explained to me, that before seeing this, though he knew about the atrocities and had recognised the bad principle, he had hesitatingly admitted the possibility that Nazi-ism was one of those degrading things through which people may be forced by circumstances to pass. This Exhibition removed any such hope from his mind: here was blasphemy against the very fact of life itself. "I shall have warmonger put on my passport," he said.

At about this time he settled on his occupation. He accepted an appointment as Press Relations Officer in the Petroleum Information Bureau, which at that time had offices in St. James's Street; and from hereon Robert's life entered a phase of unremitting activity in which I remember him easiest as a hurrying figure in a long tweed coat and a bowler hat, always tempestuously busy dashing to and from his office, to political meetings, or to conferences of the Georgian Group, or in his rooms in Swan Walk writing articles or correcting proofs with the radio roaring Beethoven at him and the cigarette always between his lips. It was still, though precariously, a happy time. War seemed by no means certain; indeed the chances seemed against it; Robert's book was now on the stalls and he felt justly proud of it, and he still had time to write a little more. When the Coronation came, Robert produced an admirable illustrated pamphlet on behalf of the Georgian Group. It was called *How We Celebrate the Coronation.* It was an attack on the individual and State vandalism, which was then, as now, denuding us of our artistic heritage. It was Robert's invective at its height, but set this time to a wholly appropriate use. In the midst of this varied existence he never forgot for an instant his major purpose. The basic theme was never lost in the fantasy of counterpoint.

Like all people made on the grand scale, Robert was conscious in a heightened degree of the obligations which individuals owe to humanity at large, obligations which he felt as personal debts of honour. In this grave matter the contrasts in his nature showed with unusual force: it was typical of him that he liked to express his deepest thoughts and convictions in terms of cynical selfishness. I remember an evening some time in the late summer of that year and Robert standing by the fire in his panelled room and expounding his ideas with characteristic under-statement. "All I am trying to do," he said, "is to remove *personal inconveniences* out of my life, nothing more than that. It's perfectly obvious that so long as one has people like the Nazis in Germany one's own life is going to be dreary and uncomfortable. One'll have to spend one's time listening to the news, digging shelters, being conscripted, that sort of thing. If I was a soldier and knew how to shoot I wouldn't mind, but as it is I've other interests, and don't want to be a soldier either. I've no ambition to walk round Buckingham Palace in a red coat and a busby, or receive medals, or even kill people. If I thought you could bribe the Nazis to leave us alone— I mean really and properly alone—well, then, I might have other views. But people who are degraded as the Nazis are have neither rudimentary honesty or free will. They are even below bribery. You can't bribe them. You know you can't. It's only politicians who believe you can." And then with a burst of indignation he added: "*I* don't want to sit in a *booth* in Trafalgar Square lecturing my fellow-citizens on what they ought to do. It's not *my* job to rouse the Empire, but no one else will." And he concluded with a comic roll of his eyes, "Except, of course, my inveterate enemies, Winston Churchill and the Pope."

In February of 1938 his brother-in-law, Ewan Butler, was appointed *Times* correspondent in Berlin. This gave Robert an additional means of finding out what was really going on. He knew very well how easy it might be to give way to emotional credence in any wild story about Germany; he was fully aware of the dangers to precise judgment from his own fierce loyalty; but from the evidence his conviction deepened rapidly. He was perplexed as to how he could adequately serve his cause. He wrote articles in the Press. He did his utmost to influence men in prominent positions whom he knew, or whom he met in the course of his work. He had a continual feeling of frustration. One of his aims was to contrive an effective machinery of libertarian propaganda, for he had estimated early in his German studies that far more influence was wielded by Dr. Goebbels than was usually supposed. But in those days propaganda of any kind was thought wicked in England. It was carelessly supposed that recourse to it was equivalent to trafficking in falsehood. Robert found himself the centre of much stupid disapproval, as the man with the bell usually does among sleepy people. The age of appeasement had arrived and Robert did not fit into it very well.

As the year advanced, as the gloomiest prophecies came to be fulfilled, Robert's sense of frustration became more and more oppressive to him. He became a Cato, preaching resistance where and how he could, and, like others uttering the same warning he seemed to be speaking to the idle winds.

Historians of the future will surely be perplexed by the phenomenon of England in those days. Explanations can be offered; none of them seem adequate. The events of the succeeding years proved that the quality of the English people had not deteriorated, yet at that period they seemed to be at the last stage of decline. Is one to believe that a degenerate puritanism had fastened on us? It is certain that a major element in our diseased state was an uneasy conscience. Scruples and sloth make happy bedfellows. The Nazis were already steeped in the blood of innocents and were turning hungry eyes on the vulnerable British Empire, yet English people continued to be so preoccupied with their own guilt in the bloodshed of the last war that they deemed it sinful to cast the first stone. That we were rich seemed to us infamous, that we ruled an Empire seemed embarrassingly wicked, that we had a minute army and a large navy seemed heavy charges against our pretensions to be a virtuous state. England, threatened with swift destruction, remained pacifist.

I saw Robert one day in July of 1938, when the threat of war over Czechoslovakia was hanging heavily over the world, and he told me that he was going to Germany as the guest of the German Government in order to attend the Nazi Party rally in Nuremberg. "I want to see the enemy for myself," he told me, "and do a little warmongering."

In her book, *Looking for Trouble*, Miss Virginia Cowles records how she met Robert on this occasion, and I may make my story coherent by quoting her extremely well-observed account of Robert in one of the oddest situations in which he ever found himself.

"The most fashionable gathering-place in Nuremberg was the Grand Hotel. Here the Parteitag's *Ehrengaeste* were housed. Usually they consisted of prominent foreigners from all over the world, but this year the French were conspicuous by their absence and only twenty or thirty English people were present. They included a sprinkling of peers eager for an Anglo-German alliance, but for the most part were

Fascist-minded Britons, members of the Mosley Party.

"Outstanding in the English group were Lord and Lady Redesdale and their daughter, the Honourable Unity Valkyrie Mitford. Unity was a tall Junoesque girl, with shoulder-length blonde curls and large blue eyes. She worshipped Hitler with a schoolgirl passion, and had persuaded her mother and father to come to Germany with her to see for themselves how wonderful he was. . . .

"Besides bringing her family with her, Unity had also invited Robert Byron to Nuremberg. This gave the group an even more curious complexion, for there was certainly no more rabid anti-Nazi than Robert. . . . I had known Robert in London, and during the week we frequently wandered about the town and visited the beer-gardens together. Robert had come to Nuremberg out of curiosity and was undecided as to whether the show was comic or sinister.

"'These people are so grotesque,' he kept on saying. 'If we go to war, it will be like fighting a gigantic zoo.'

"Robert maintained a light vein but at times his indignation got the better of him. I remember one afternoon when we went into the Wurttemberger Hof for tea. The restaurant was crowded with officials, all of whom seemed in a very jolly frame of mind, laughing and talking loudly. Seated at the next table were Dr. Silex, editor of the Deutsche Allgemeine Zeitung, Dr. Dietrich the Press chief, Dr. von Dircksen the German Ambassador to London, and Herr von Loesch of the Foreign Office. They invited us to join them, and soon the conversation turned inevitably to the topics of the day. Dr. Silex referred to the article in the London *Times* (of September 7th in which it was suggested that the Czechs might solve their difficulties by ceding Sudetenland to Germany) and said he was sure England would come to her senses before it was too late, and realise that Czechoslovakia was not the concern of Britain but of Germany. I saw a red flush rising on Robert's neck and the next moment I heard him saying in a deadly voice, ' What happens on the Continent is always England's concern. Every now and again we are unfortunate enough to be led by a Chamberlain—but that's only temporary. Don't be misguided. In the end we *always* rise up and oppose the tyrannies that threaten Europe. We have smashed them before, and I warn you we will smash them again.' A terrible silence fell, then Herr von Loesch laughed uneasily and suggested that we talk of ' less serious things.' The conversation was strained, and when we got up to leave no one urged us to stay."

It is still early to estimate the necessity, wisdom, or pusillanimity of the Munich Accord. In England the issue is still confused by the organised hysteria of party politics, and in the world at large it may remain open for many years to come. All that I need say for the purposes of this essay is that Robert took the extremest imaginable anti-Munich view. To him the episode, being neither necessary or excusable, was the most abominable betrayal recorded in English history. When I met him again at the end of September he was in a state of desperation such as I had never seen him in before. He told me that what had most impressed him was the consternation with which Germans whom he had met had learned from him that England was ready and anxious to fight them, and now by giving them a needless victory we had given them unaccustomed self-confidence. (Of course Robert, like everyone else then, overestimated our strength in arms.)

"If you'd *seen* them," he said, "I spent hours with storm-troopers and S.S. men and the rest, and they poured beer and hock down my throat and pawed me like great blubbering bears. They longed to be loved. Do you know those sort of Germans who are tall and look like wolves with eczema? There was one, an S.S.

officer, and when I said to him in a beer-garden: ' It's fun here, what a pity we'll all be shooting each other soon,' he went pale, his lip quivered, and he burst out tearfully: ' Ach no, ve are all off oss zo much kounting that Englandt vill not be war upon oss making also.' He nearly wept. I admit he was drunk. But now, God damn and curse it, he's right and I'm wrong."

Although, as usual, Robert expressed himself jestingly, he looked as though he had passed through some shattering personal tragedy. He paced round the room as he talked, often uttering exclamations of disgust, or stopped and sighed angrily. And yet his horror at what was then going forward increased rather than limited the fascinated interest with which he contemplated insane Germany. He told me about the Nazi hierarchy. I knew Hitler and Goebbels by sight but none of the others. "Oh, you ought to see Goering!" he cried; "he's the best of the lot. He's a little tub, with smooth skin and layers of make-up on his face. Himmler isn't worth looking at, nor is Ribbentrop, but Hess is a marvellous specimen." Mentioning a swarthy friend of ours, he added: "If X. turned into an animal, like Nebuchadnezzar, he'd look like Hess about half-way through the process." He showed me a toy car he had bought. It was a reproduction in miniature of Hitler's sacred vehicle, and was equipped with four dolls to scale representing the Führer and his chief henchmen. He used to run the toy car round and round his table. Never did Robert lose his queer individual humour and fun, but now the comic manner in which he expressed himself showed like flashes of gaiety against the deep sadness of his habitual thoughts. He was full of "those odd tricks which sorrow shoots out of the mind." It was with relief that he left England in October for an official three months' tour of American oil-fields.

Robert's life from henceforth was so much bound up with his political interests, interests which he pursued as before, through his official occupation, through meetings, through journalism, and through the badgering—

it is the correct word—of complacent Ministers, under-secretaries, members of all parties, and his friends, into a realisation that a climax of civilisation was at hand; so closely did the events of his career follow the succession of horrible events that led to the war, that a chronological recital of them does not seem necessary. Let the reader bear in mind the background: the renewed anti-Semitic persecution in November of 1938, the seizure of Prague in March of the following year, the beginning of the Polish crisis in the summer, the Conscription debate in the House of Commons, the declaration of war in September, and I will recall some facts and incidents to illustrate Robert's penultimate period, the period which, in spite of its occasional confusion, was made coherent by the pure virtue of his loyalty.

He was in London for a week in December of 1938 before going to spend Christmas with his sister Lucy and her husband Ewan Butler in Berlin. One night we dined together at Whites, and he told me that his chief aim in going to Germany was to explain to any influential Germans he met the reasons why Nazi policy must bring about war with England. The brief escape to America, while it had intensified his disgust with Munich through making him aware of American opinion on that matter, had given him sufficient rest to restore calm to his mind.

"I want to tell the Germans," he said, "that with us honour is mixed up with economics. One reason why we are champions of the rule of law is that it is our only way of keeping income tax down. How on earth could we afford to protect our communications in a world where pledges and treaties were not honoured? Of course we couldn't, and that is the reason why we fight for treaties, even minor ones, and other peoples. I don't believe any one has told the Germans that. I am always surprised how few English politicians know about our simple position in the world. You hear people say that we always fight a Power that becomes dominantly powerful on the Continent. What rubbish! As though

we fought Napoleonic France just because it happened to
be great! English Ministers and publicists spread that
idea and with it a notion of our meanness. We fight
lawlessness. We fight tyrannies, because they always are
lawless and threaten us implicitly. We generally try not
to fight them, but we can't help ourselves. I'll tell the
Germans that. It's why I'm going."

That conversation remained as a strong impression
in my mind. I think I have given his words exactly.

From this visit to Germany—a Germany now insolent
with success and openly hostile to us whom they were
being taught to despise—he returned to an England sunk
deeper in inertia. The sighs of relief uttered over Munich
had turned into snores of complacency. Optimism was
the order of the day.

Although Robert had been interested since boyhood
in political questions, politics, in the narrower sense,
bored him. He often said that he regarded ideal Government as a humdrum work-a-day function of supplying
necessities and mitigating the injustices of Fortune, unobtrusively. He never thought very seriously of becoming
a parliamentary candidate. But for the first time, now,
under pressure of exasperation and anger, he began to
identify his political sympathies, and to my surprise he
found himself drawn towards a world which he had long
known through scholarly interests, but with which he
had, I think, very little in common—namely, the extreme
Left intelligentsia. It was an odd partnership, though it
had a logical reason for existence. It seemed to Robert
that the leaders of England, the ruling party of conservative business men, were not only ignorant of
England's historical duty, but were so small-souled that
they were willing to barter it for trifling selfish advantages. Among his extremist friends he found sympathy with this point of view. Among them he appeared
as a moderate, which, in other respects, he essentially
was. And so among them, in consequence, he felt so
much more at ease than with other people that it was

only rarely that he realised what a queer world they formed. Their philosophy of life was a crazy hotch-potch of contradictory convictions: they believed in pacifism, revolutionary bloodshed, puritanism, and license, all at the same time. They were mostly learned men with little experience of the ordinary world, suffering from psychological disorders and mental indigestion; but here, in this violent-minded world, Robert found the absence of the vice he most abhorred in England: complacency. Nor was there then any party or faction of them which was prepared to ignore the crimes of Nazi-ism for the sake of a little ignoble quiet. There was another reason too: Robert's self-possessed calm was rapidly leaving him again. With an increase of emotionalism he was prepared to believe in the mythology of the Left, that bogeyland of blood-drinking bankers and business men evoked from the ultra-economic theory of history, because this suited his detestation of the party of Neville Chamberlain so well.

I used often to argue with him over his new political orientation, and several times he answered me in these words: "They're anti-Nazis. I feel safe with them."

The last months before the war were spent by Robert in a continual battle. He became more violent in his behaviour than he had ever been before; he lay about him on all sides, and the number of his victims grew to be large. I got into some trouble myself. It may be remembered that an Arab-Zionist conference was called in the early spring of that year with the object of settling the Palestinian problem. Coming of a family with Palestinian traditions, I became somewhat involved in this event. I wrote several articles for the Press and was used as a stage property for some of the entertainments in honour of the Arabian princes. Robert was a strong Zionist; I took the opposite view. I never expressed anti-Semitic views, I endeavoured to present myself as a pro-Semite with anti-Zionist opinions; in fact I urged the unpopular suggestion that England rather than Palestine should be a scene of unlimited Jewish immigration. In Robert's eyes, however, these views brought me near to treachery to the anti-Nazi cause. He rang me up one morning to tell me that I was a "hooded horror," and soon after, varying the "Crag" theme, my wife and I became known to him as the "Cags," this appellation being short for "Cagoulard." I enjoyed this controversy enormously; it was in the best of our Persian coffee-house traditions, and no bones were broken. But there were other far more serious quarrels.

Robert belonged to a distinguished dining-club in London where he used to meet many of the eminent men of the day. Most of his friends there were of the same opinion as himself; it was a place (there is no indiscretion in saying so now) where members of the House of Commons used to vent their rage against the inadequacy of their then leadership, but among the members of this club there were some strong Municheers as well. One of these, holding an extremely important position at that time, came in for an unexpected toss from Robert when without knowing it he showed a red rag. Not long after the seizure of Prague, Robert was dining at this club (where, since dinner was served at one table, conversation had a habit of becoming general), when this member began to discuss a speech recently delivered by the Prime Minister. Not aware of the frantic resentment he was arousing in one member of his audience, he went on to pay some extravagant compliments to the architect of appeasement. He paused for breath. Robert leaned across the table and asked him a question. He did not seem to hear. He felt he must have heard wrong. He continued his dissertation and paused again. Robert again leaned across the table and again asked the same question: "Are you in German pay?"

This time it was said very clearly.

I witnessed another devastating attack on another man bearing a well-known name. It occurred after a dinner-party while the men were sitting in the dining-room over their port. Conversation had turned to the ever-present topic of the day. Two eminent guests were sitting at the top of the table, Sacheverell Sitwell and myself were sitting on their left, Robert was alone on the other side. It was obvious as soon as one of the eminent men declared his faith in the ability of the Government to handle the approaching crisis that there would be a scuffle. There was some open sparring to begin with, until Robert, having dealt massive blows on both, fastened with all his grim anger on the one next to Sitwell. I can hear his "deadly voice" now.

"What you mean," he said, "is that in spite of Munich, in spite of everything that's happened since that surrender, in spite of all the passes being sold, you still believe in a British guarantee."

"Yes, I do," replied the other hotly.

Robert filled his glass with port. "I'd like very much," he went on, "to have you under a glass case with a pin stuck through you. I'd have a label tied round your neck. I'd show you to people with strong stomachs. A perfect specimen of the British ruling class to-day."

If Sitwell had not intervened they might have come to blows. Afterwards, when Robert learned to his consternation that he had misdirected his fire in this instance, he sent his victim a handsome apology. I met the victim a few days later. "What an extraordinary man Byron is," he said; "the first time I met him he treated me like a tramp and then sent me a very nice letter."

These are some of the incidents I remember, but the main fact I remember is that of a man persistently haunted by the monstrosities which his clear vision could not allow him to disregard for a single second. There is a point where heightened intelligence incurs anguish, where the too-seeing eye and the too-sensitive ear inflict sometimes unendurable pain. Many great artists and men of abnormally capacious mind have paid this price for the bounty of the gods, and I believe that Robert, endowed as few are, belonged in his later days to this enviable though often unhappy company. He would underestimate the rare character of his sensibility, and so he would often mistake for deliberate treachery the ability of other people to find solace in sleepy escapism.

At the end of the summer he went to stay with my sister and brother-in-law in Northern Ireland. He was there in the last month of peace, and with them he heard Neville Chamberlain's broadcast speech on the 3rd of September announcing a state of war between Great Britain and Germany. My sister told me that when the broadcast was over he poured himself out a drink and made the following observation: " Well, there's one thing to be thankful for: the post-war decadence ought to be even better than the last one." He returned to London immediately.

I met Robert shortly after, at a time which, I believe, to have been the unhappiest of his whole life. In that gloomy mood of anti-climax in which England went to war, he had found an added anti-climax in his inability to find war-work. He had been led to expect an appointment in which he could put his knowledge and ability to a full use. But the appointment was not forthcoming. At the end of September he accepted an offer from the B.B.C. to become a sub-editor in the Overseas News Department. I have a memory of that time, of myself arriving at his rooms early one evening, and of him arriving some five minutes after me with the slow step and drawn weary expression of an ill man. He greatly envied my brother and me, then in the farcical position of being elderly and bewildered lieutenants in the army. He asked me to help him to join the army. He said it would be fun if we could serve in the same battalion.

He asked me to do this for him several times, and every time I argued strongly against it and I think persuaded him. It seemed to me that a man with such gifts, and such specialised knowledge, would be wasted as an army officer. That was my thought then, but now that I know more of the life of public affairs and of the life of the army in war, I feel differently. I think a man like Robert might have been totally wasted in a political department, while I can imagine him as an extremely effective fighting officer. He would have found the habits of discipline and command unnatural to him at first, no doubt, but he was the kind of man whom men would follow. He meant what he said, and he had moral and physical courage. He might have found the perfect opening in some of the auxiliary and inventive types of warfare which were evolved towards the end, and which required men of imagination. Such might well have been his ultimate career in the war. But he was incalculable.

We met again when I was posted to a staff appointment in London in the early Spring of 1940. He had now passed through and overcome that hateful ordeal of the spirit which I had witnessed last, and during which his worn nerves and exhausted vitality had brought him near to a delusion of persecution. I think I was instrumental in terminating that period. I had found out that his violent behaviour, which had not been free of indiscretion, in the year preceding the war had earned him much disapproval in high places. I told him bluntly why he had been refused the expected first-rate appointments. I had hated telling him this unpalatable truth and had expected an explosion of wrath. To my surprise he received this news with relief: he knew now where he was, and the natural resilience of his spirits began immediately to assert itself once more. Unlike some of the people in power, he was never a man to harbour resentment for its own sake. As the war moved to its first climax he threw himself into his work with his natural animation, unconscious as yet of the incurable (and perhaps lovable) ineptitude of British administration in the arts of propaganda, unconscious as yet that he might be wasting his time. He had entirely recovered his self-possession, and his abounding spirits in that hag-ridden time were an inestimable boon to those who saw him. And it is thus, with all his wit and fighting optimism at its height, that I last remember him. We parted at midnight on the 30th of May. I went to Egypt the next morning. We never met again.

Sometime toward the end of September his friend, Mrs. Otto Khan, who was then in Cairo, showed me a letter from him in which he told her of the extraordinary exhilaration of spirits which he, like some others, had experienced during the bombardments. "I would not have missed the experience," he said, "of one afternoon, watching from a window in a London club, while the future of the world (I choose my words carefully) was being decided in the sky above us."

About a month later I heard from him.

"MY DEAR CRAG,

"I envy you being in the Middle East. I have hopes of getting there myself but it is not easily arranged. I don't know when we'll meet again.

"You would not believe what this country has been like. I stayed with Richard in Dover the other day while cross channel fire was going on, and it gave one an epic feeling. It is a pity in a way that you have missed it. You would have enjoyed it like I did. Of course a great deal of damage has been done, and in more than one way we have been saved by our gift for improvisation. That's where our vile amateurishness comes in so usefully.

"Our propaganda machinery has more or less broken down completely. This is very embittering to the few of us who have been working for years to contrive a voice for ourselves. It's pretty well past repair now.

"I don't know when we shall meet. Probably some time next year in Egypt. I'm told Napoleon Basket[1] is with you. Has he forgiven us?

              "Yours ever,

                  "ROBERT."

[1] A senior British official, who was libelled by us under this name in *Innocence and Design.*

F.S.L.

This letter remained unanswered for a long time. One day early in 1941 I was thinking that I must write to Robert when I was told by a friend of ours, recently arrived from England, that Robert had left the B.B.C. and must even then have started out for Egypt. He was coming as a Special Correspondent for a group of English newspapers. Later I heard more from other people in the course of G.H.Q. gossip. Various departments were anxious to enlist his services; there was some competition for them; there was no reason why he should not be a Special Correspondent and hold other appointments as well. I could not resist a smile. His destination, secret as such matters always were in the war, was so blatantly obvious. His name was Byron and the battle of Greece was drawing near.

We had grown used, in Cairo, to long delays in arrivals from England. It never occurred to me to grow anxious as the weeks followed each other and there was still no sign. It was not till the early Summer, when Ewan Butler arrived, that the dreadful possibility of what had happened became suddenly clear. Ewan was astonished to find that he had not arrived. I sent a telegram to my wife, and she told me that all hope was now abandoned. His boat had been torpedoed. There were no survivors.

In this essay I have set down a personal recollection of Robert Byron. If my description is one-sided, that is because I have drawn almost exclusively on my own experiences. There was much else in his life on which I have not touched; there remains much more to be said, I hope elsewhere, than I have said here. But I hope I have said enough to convey to any reader of these pages some notion of what was lost in him. Let me take my recollections a little further.

It was only now that he had gone that I realised how great a place he had filled in my affections, and how much had been taken away. To be afflicted by grief in a crowd is intolerable, so I sought an opportunity to be alone. I found it one early morning in Gezira, when an image of his life came without effort before my mind. What a treasure-house of experience that life contained! What a multitude of men, countries, minds, and adventures he had known! There is such a thing as self-indulgence in the nobler pleasures. There are people who besot themselves with the joys of adventure. Though he had lived more intensely than any other man I had known, he was far from any such charge, and I seemed to see the answer to this challenge in one fact: that though he bore little resemblance to his great namesake and kinsman, they resembled each other in this: both their lives had been as abundantly illuminated by great devotions to great causes. He had lived on the wise maxim that the world is the possession of those who do not want to keep it to themselves. Insistent pain came from one reflection: Robert had died at the age of thirty-six. By the old ideas of the span of human life he had lived only half his natural years, and by modern ideas less than that. By any calculation he had lived far less than a third of his expectable life as a grown man. So his ambitions were all left unfulfilled. Surely the spectacle of a conscious design, such as was in Robert's life, destroyed when so incomplete, could only allow for indignant regret, and for nothing more. A hundred times No! This was an absolute misrepresentation. The more I thought about Robert's life the more it filled me with a sense of exhilaration. How many lives, even such as are considered to be distinguished and admirable, could compare in the quality of action with this fragment of a life? And surely, I thought then, and still think, Robert was a man to be envied profoundly rather than pitied, because, for all the tragedy of his young death, he had already achieved the greatest of all ambitions: a life which was tremendously worth living.

4

IN TIMES OF STRESS

> To be worst,
> The lowest and most dejected thing of fortune,
> Stands still in esperance.
>
> KING LEAR.

LIKE MANY other Englishmen, I knew France before
the war as a convenient acquaintance rather than as
a friend. I had got much of my education there, I
spoke the language, and if I may illustrate what I mean
by "convenience," so as to clear it of any suggestion of
rudeness, let me say that I had once migrated to Paris for a
year in order to write a book, because there, surrounded
as nowhere else by a splendid and yet matter-of-fact pride
in culture, I had found a comfortable and inspiring
atmosphere in which to work. But though France had
often seemed to me Europe at its most fine and ordered,
I felt only a distant affection, indeed I avoided intimacy.
I argued that there was a whole world's difference between
recognition of virtues and the choice of a life's partner,
between respect and love, and further, that to attempt
intimacy between elements so immensely different as
English and French temperaments, traditions, whatever
makes up character, was to invite distressing failure. Let
the relationship, rather, be confined to those arts of
superficial joyous companionship in which no people in
the world are more apt than the French; let the everyday
commerce of soul and mind be so delightfully restrained
as to leave the more serious fabric of esteem out of peril.

I dare say that for those days, when Montparnasse was
still haunted by English, Americans and Germans
attempting a fatuous imitation of French life and
manners, for the miserable bitter years of the 'thirties

when France and England in alliance were more like two fear-stricken and puzzled invalids than the champions of civilisation, my planned frivolity was not a contemptible solution; but I believed that I had formulated an axiom, and that there were deep reasons which proscribed an attempt at deeper initiations. The magnitude of this error was made plain to me much later, towards the end of the war. It was then, during the winter and spring preceding the invasion, that I worked with a group of French officers in England and that I learned not only that the famed exclusiveness of the French temperament was a myth based on as little reality as the legendary pointed top hat and imperial beard, but that no people in the world are more generous or more sincere in the conduct of serious friendship. This was a prelude to the proofs we saw of the majestic strength of French firmness of soul, the sincerity of French loyalty in stress, danger and pain. Let me, in token of gratitude, remember now the names of Guy de Roquebrunne and Roger de la Grandière.

In the last winter of the war I spent a long evening in talk with a French friend in London. He and I had just come back from France, and we were discussing together the widely various and excessively numerous impressions which we had brought back from the military operations, and I, in addition, from my later visit to Lorraine. I complained to him, at one moment, that as a writer I was placed in a thoroughly uncomfortable position, rather like that of an amateur of food and wine who had been forcibly fed and compulsorily made drunk with so great an excess of experience on my hands that rather than be able to select, my capacity for digestion might be permanently impaired. In sympathy he offered me melancholy comfort by reminding me how quickly, and how tragically, experiences of violence become obliterated from conscious memory. Towards the end of the evening I told him of a remark made to me by an Alsatian peasant woman which had amused me. She had explained German success over France in

the following words: "Vous savez comment c'était,
Monsieur, les Français sont trop bons et trop bêtes."
Now, I said, I had heard a great many descriptions of
French character in my time but never that, and I found
it in wonderfully absurd contradiction to all known facts
in the case. Much to my surprise my friend saw nothing
funny in the remark. "I don't say I agree," he said, "with
her explanation, but it was not a shallow or an unthinking
remark. Don't you see that simplicity, respect for convention, trust (foolish at moments) are the real foundations on which French character is built. All the clever
things about France which you know, all the perversity,
amorality, and silliness which strike you in the eye,
might hide that fact from you for ever. But you ask
Frenchmen." He ended by saying: "I believe your
Alsatian gave you the stomach powder to help you to
digest your banquet."

I have never been able to agree with my friend, or
with other Frenchmen to whom I repeated the Alsatian
woman's remark, that "too much goodness and stupidity"
are dangerous French failings, but I was impressed at the
uniformity of intelligent French reaction to my tale.
Though I had, in a way, been led by intimacy to my
starting-point, having received profound confirmation of
what I had first learned from de Tocqueville, namely
that the French character is extreme, flexible, and incalculable, I reflected that perhaps, as with the ancient
Greeks, the character persisted, because it was so firmly
poised on an enduring simplicity and on a recognition
that certain things should be changeless. And it occurred
to me, too, that without having searched for it, I had seen
something of that essential France, face to face, in some
of the blackest days of her history.

In this essay I do not wish to give a recital of military
events, but to consider the interplay of character and
situation as I saw it in a French town, a town I must say
now, to which I and my companions owe a debt of

gratitude which can never be repayed. To make my story easily understood, however, let me, in two paragraphs, indicate what were the general circumstances of Lorraine when these things happened.

In the early autumn of 1944 Eastern France had been reduced to a state of helplessness in which the bare hope of survival was the animating force of men's lives. At the end of August the Allied Armies had not yet reached the Moselle, but their advance had been held nowhere since the break-through, and in the Vosges highlands (where my town lies) the people hoped that at the last moment, in the week or so remaining to them, there would be such a rising of the Maquis that the longed-for liberation would not occur in the humiliating way of charity, but, partly at least, as an act of French defiance and revenge. Of course, these hopes were doomed.

In mid-August a small force from my regiment parachuted into the Vosges; at the end of August reinforcements (including myself) dropped to them and the Maquis. We were greeted by a host of untrained, unarmed, expectant, and physically exhausted young men, whose only idea of military formation was to assemble in large masses, whose strategy consisted in firing what few weapons they possessed at every rustle of a rabbit, or in shouting their passwords from wood to wood, and into whose ranks traitors had been introduced. Within a few days the inevitable disaster took place. They were routed by the Germans, who killed nearly a third of them and fatally demoralised the rest. After the first week of September there were but the remnants of a Maquis in the Vosges, and my regiment found itself with a re-formed fragment of these shattered forces whom at the last moment they had been able to rescue. At the same moment the American armies were halted on the Moselle. The people, who had expected to welcome American soldiers in a matter of days, had to wait now for nearly three months. We, the English troops, were faced with a new problem: we had to find an area free from " the grey lice" (as the Germans were called) where we could receive our armed transport and equipment, and then attack. To achieve this we had to rely on the people of a certain town in the middle of the Vosges, to whose immense conifer forests we had secretly migrated.

The heroics, the stirring deeds, the reckless gallantry in battle of French resistance I never saw. I have no doubt that every word of praise these things received was nobly earned, but the soil on which these fine blooms of courage grew was the ordinary, familiar, ancient life of France, whose strength is as esoteric as it is terrific, which is as flexible in stress as it is firmly rooted, and which I did see persisting amid sufferings which might have been thought overwhelming.

How difficult it is, even so soon after as now, to recall that disgusting Life-in-Death which the Germans imposed in the place of real living nature. With what weariness, with what a feeling of staleness and boredom, one now hears the names of the Gestapo, of the Sicherheitsdienst, of the S.S., and all the rest of the sickening catalogue. This emotion we in England connect with post-war reaction, but something of it was always part of the nightmare; it is also a natural reaction of " health" to " disease," of sanity to madness, and in France it was very visible in the midst of the danger. The French were bored to death with the Germans. They were so bored that they could not be bothered to take precautions against them. It was the outward sign of their greater inner strength, their fast ebbing but greater strength. This French moral superiority, built upon a simple and absolute conviction that on their side was a great right and on the German side only a detestable wrong, has often been remarked on and described; but its most surprising though most natural manifestation was a heavy insistence on ordinary life. I can best explain what I mean by saying that this scrupulous normality in life, which in days of police supervision had provided safety, had incurred a poetry of defiance, and after the passage of long bitter years became wrapped up in something like ritual significance. The point must not be over-emphasised if for no other reason than that it was so often obscured, but it was a central fact of French resistance.

"The art of our necessities is strange."

It was this that gave an unexpected and moving significance to the cycle of work, recreation, church, and the day-to-day life of the town, which we could see as we looked from our forest hiding-place into the deep dark green valleys of the Vosges. The sound of the squeaking and lumbering forester's wagons had a rare and, to us, then, inexplicable poignancy.

The core of strength in this French life which refused to accept defeat came chiefly from the women—from those powerful middle-aged women of France. I know now what Joan of Arc would have looked like in later life if fate had been kinder to her in youth. I remember well that in England before the invasion some grave doubts had arisen as to the reliability of a certain French unit in battle: it was mutinous and corrupted by political dissension, added to which the men had said that once arrived in France they would go the quickest way home. "Don't be deceived," one of their officers said to me, "when they see French women they'll fight like tigers." I thought at the time that his remark was facetious, but I now know why he made it, and its great truth. These women, above all, didn't give a damn for the Germans. Helpless as they were, by the sheer force of personality they kept the invaders at bay and recklessly led and cheered on any one who bore arms on the right side. It would not have been easy to give way to panic in front of them. They unnerved the Germans. They were queens of truculence and back-chat, and when they did services for the Germans, as sometimes they had to, they did so in a manner which did not allay the enemy's disquiet. But as a rule the Germans kept their distance—that is to say, they either turned them out of their houses and lived there by themselves, or else they left these women and their houses strictly alone.   The truculence was so very overwhelming. I know well what I am talking about, as once when I had to visit one of our "Madames" at midnight I was mistaken by her for a German.

Their loudly expressed contempt for "les salauds" was not without disadvantages. They had little sense of that odious necessity of war, "security," to maintain which they had simple, over-simple, rules. Not a word except a highly misleading one was ever spoken about our military dispositions to the Germans, but our place in that stressed ordinary life led to many mad risks, as did, on occasion, their own strong-voiced feelings about the war. They liked entertaining us to enormous celebration lunches and dinners; it was often difficult not to sit through meals the size of banquets without appearing rude, in spite of the fact that the Germans were in the town.   Perhaps my most dramatic memory of the war is of passing the open door of a house, on a rainy night when the North, South, and Eastern horizons were intermittently bright with gun-flashes, through which issued the strains of the "Marseillaise" from a rusted gramophone, and a loud female voice taking up a line "A bas les Doryphores!" (the potato-bug, another nick-name for the Germans).

Madame Rossi, who lived in a tall, shuttered house on the road, about half a mile from our town, was an archetype of our protectresses. Her physical appearance suggested ponderous immobility, while her loud laughing voice, which filled the room like a coaching-horn blown indoors, gave but a slight indication of her indomitable vitality. She was as persistently merry in the face of danger as though she actually relished it: my memory of her is always first of loud hearty peasant laughter. She was exposed to far more danger than most, she had had far more distressful experiences, and this because she was not the type who is made for subterfuge; the Germans knew well enough that this large, full-bosomed, fair-haired mirthful woman was their bitter enemy. Her house was on a little subsidiary road which left the town for an adjoining valley running, as they all did, between immense pine-clad mountains, and its situation was near one of the few mountain paths which led to the darkness of the forest and to our probable hiding-place. Visits by Gestapo agents were frequent, and before I arrived in the second party her house had been searched while she had six of our men hidden. It is not difficult to imagine how such experiences can wrack the toughest nerves. But Madame Rossi never gave a sign of a twinge. She never suggested that her house should no longer be used as a refuge and a rendezvous. "O la! les Boches!" she would cry as she leaned against her kitchen table with red arms crossed and her blue eyes rolling. "Boh! Those filthy creatures! They're brutes, that's what they are." Then she would laugh; not ironically, just at the whole crazy business. I think it is not extravagant to say that her sense of humour was not, as with most other people, an affair of jokes and comic surprises, but went down deep in her nature. She was terrifically sane.

The first time I met her happened as follows. As I approached the house in the dark with my colonel, we were held up by two melodramatic figures with pistols. Recognitions were whispered and arms lowered. There was an agent abroad—it was all right, the house was surrounded by sentries. When we knocked we heard a hushed pandemonium within, and the daughter, a hillock compared to the mountainous mother, but of great proportion and trumpet-tongued as she was, looked out carefully, and, recognising us, beckoned us in. We found Madame in her favourite pose by the table, and then the pandemonium recommenced, as it were in reverse order, doors opening and shutting all round as in an old-fashioned French farce, while the local Maquis Commander emerged with other hidden beings. The agent

was described in detail by the daughter: how he had
come into the house, looked round with a hideous snarl,
spoken with a heavy German accent and wore a black cap.
The black cap gave me an idea and I drew a pencil sketch
of a Maquisard lately arrived in the district—yes, it was
he.   There was a general gasp of relief, and the sentries
were called in for a drink.   And when they were sitting
down drinking Mirabelle out of little glasses, Madame
spared a moment from her cooking to fairly scold them
for their false alarm.   "Frightening honest women like
that—*Mon Dieu!* because a man's face frightens you,"
and heaping abuse on them, she ended up by falling
forward on the table and laughing till both she and the
table quivered together.   "Tu es un imbecile!" she gasped
between roars of merriment.   Someone suggested we
should be quieter, as the Germans—and "*Mon* . . .! les
Salauds!" shouted Madame as she bore the omelette to
the table.

I never saw her downcast, even at the darkest moments:
she was always ready to house and to feed soldiers and slap
them on the back and tell them they were heroes when
they felt more like lost dogs.   She was, as I say, the type
of the resistance, and her grandeur of character bore a
classic hall-mark: she was not conscious of being remarkable.   After the war I visited her to get her to fill
up a form which would enable her to receive the King's
Medal, and as she placed a hand on my shoulder, fairly
weighing me down where I sat explaining the details,
"Mais non!" she broke in, rolling her blue eyes, "Voyez
—ça n'est pas pour moi, c'est pour les militaires, ça."
There was no affectation.   I asked her what had
happened to her after our departure.   "The Boches were
always around the house," she said.   "They guessed all
right.   So one day I called out to their sergeant: ' Hi,
you,' I said, ' are you looking for billets for your men?
Come in here.   I have plenty of room and plenty of hay.'
They went."   I can imagine how she uttered that
invitation.

There were many such gay stout-hearted women in the Vosges, but I must not allow an impression that such beings were a majority, or that, though these merry-makers were the strength and the spring of defiance, the nightmare was anything but insupportable. Fear was a daily companion. It is difficult even for a soldier to imagine the intensity of such unremitting drawn-out ordeals of fear which French people suffered for five years; the fear of death in battle is little compared to what is engendered by the helplessness of immobility and remorseless hostile scrutiny. I know of two women who, during the brief time we were in the Vosges, went mad. I know of another who very nearly went mad, but was able to save herself by the same strict self-discipline by which she had quelled to great purpose five years of fear.

Mlle. Bergeron was the antithesis of Madame Rossi: a severe, conventional, serious, middle-aged spinster who kept a small farm out in the country. The Germans knew she was frightened and suspected that she was working for the Maquis and us. How they hated her! I think they hated her more than any of the others, and for a not obscure reason: she seemed such a prize within their grasp, she was the principal message-bearer of the whole Maquis organisation, and there were few things they wanted to know which she could not have told. But she never gave in. They heaped every humiliation on her to break her spirit, to break the spirit of this obviously terrified woman, and they failed absolutely. They made her house into a brothel, they beat her, they tortured her, with no avail. This quiet, prim, very ordinary looking, well-dressed woman had the strength of a tiger. Their final revenge is too disgusting to describe. In the same house there lived her invalid aunt, about eighty years old. On the last night that the Germans were in the Vosges they dragged this wretched old woman out of her bed and made her dance for them in her nightgown. She died. Then they smashed up the house, and left.

There was one "ange de la résistance" in a near-by village who, as I look back, seems almost to spoil my picture, to bring a note of over-popular romance into the hard realism of my gallery of modern Joans. She was a young girl of eighteen, with bright fair hair, beautiful features, and for all her grace the strength of a man; she was, in fact, Joan of Arc much as popular fancy would have her, but such as an astute stage manager might reject on the grounds that she did not fulfil the requirement of plainness. If Mlle. Bergeron illustrates the darker, the more true aspect of resistance, this adorable creature may stand as a symbol for the occasional and no less real element of romance which occasionally as by a flash illuminated the hateful scene. I knew her by repute, as she guided another company of our re-inforcements across the forests south of Baccarat and across the river Meurthe to join us in the Vosges high-lands. Her beauty, her incredible endurance, her courage and her wonders on the march, how she leaped down precipitous stream-beds from crag to crag, had often been told to me, so that when after the war I went to pay her an official visit of thanks, I was in much curiosity. Mlle. Simone was exactly as she had been described, and when later she conducted me through the woods to a neigh-bouring hamlet, I followed with as much difficulty and as many falls as though guided by some intelligent wild animal.

She had lived as a Maquisarde for two years and had enjoyed it thoroughly. She had crossed the lines, which after mid-September were static and thus very difficult to get through, some five or six times. When military information was needed about German dispositions, she took the simple course of walking to the German lines and looking. She had only one grievance—namely, that when the American Army at long last arrived in November they placed her under arrest for a few hours. I tried to calm her by explaining that as she was the only person left in her shell-shattered village when they arrived, and as the only explanation she could give them was that she wanted to see a battle, they were not wholly unreasonable in considering her with momentary suspicion. But nothing could assuage her anger or stem her torrent of protestation. She was a strong and garrulous character.

Our meeting ended in a pleasing scene. I had been charged with a set of finely printed documents—formal letters of thanks from our Brigadier to French families who had helped us in the campaign, one of which was destined for Mlle. Simone. As it was written in English, I translated it for her, without interruption until I came to a particularly solemn statement: "Vos actes de patriotisme," I read, "en ce qui concerne nos opérations sont notés par le gouvernement britannique, et seront conservés dans les archives de notre Ministère de la Guerre." At this she burst out laughing outright, and, unable myself to continue with a serious countenance, I handed it to her with the translation incomplete.

The Maquis, as I have said, had been shattered in the first week of September, yet, most strangely, it continued until mid-October to be effective. A great bluff was attempted which, with our aid, was successful. Over the whole area of the Vosges highlands, not a great area of France, but seeming very great as the huge natural barriers restrict nearly all roads to an east-west direction, the pine forests continue with hardly an interruption. The Maquis kept these forests clear of Germans, and they did this because they were untrained. This may sound like a silly paradox, but it is the truth: having no conception of what is called "fieldcraft," they always let their presence be known. They continued to fire their weapons at every starting rabbit or hare, and the result was that at widely separated points the crackle of automatic guns was heard every day. This simple evidence persuaded the Germans that the Maquis were an immense and heavily armed force, and in consequence they did not dare enter the woods till October. This allowed a few remnants of the Maquis and ourselves to fight with the essential, though never delightful, consolation of somewhere safe in the woods to return to. Had these untrained, underfed boys been able to stay till the end of November in the wretched cold of the woods, it is possible that the Germans would never have dared enter them at all. The fault which cost so many of them their lives was that they became too ready to come into the towns and swagger, not bothering about agents or spies. Some large captures were made, and, of course, some of them broke down under torture and told the truth about their companions.

Of the active Maquisards, the one whom I saw most often was Albert, the Garde de Chasse, or, as he would be called in English, the State Gamekeeper of the place. He was the principal intelligence officer of the Maquis, and therefore my colleague, my opposite number. We met daily by a certain tree. Albert was a gloomy, hard, egotistical, passionately patriotic, passionately loyal man. Weeks of shared misery made us life-long friends. He was of slight build, sandy-haired, invariably wearing gaiters, a beret, and the rough tweed cloak which Alsatians share with Germans, and of his many intensely French characteristics it was his dry pedantry which was most immediately noticeable. As we stood together in that incessant Vosgian drizzle of rain under our tree, he would expound to me the movements and dispositions of the Germans in an elegantly-expressed, well-constructed academic oration. When I broke in with a "No, listen, we came across such and such yesterday——" "Attendez," he would interrupt, holding up his hand, "Wait, I will come to that in a moment. To resume——" and so the lecture would go on. I never knew him to give information which was inaccurate even in details, and he always said when he did not know. He was not modest. I know other Frenchmen who, pardonably, and perfectly honourably nervous in the days of the oppression, incline to smack their chests and strut in the fashion of Chanticleer now that it is all over. But I find the post-war boastfulness of Albert acceptable, even endearing and proper, for there was no discernible difference in his conduct then (when he was the man whom of all men the Germans sought most eagerly to capture for torture and a confession), and after his liberation.

He had a devotion to his duty as a game preserver such as is common all the world over in his profession. He was also a man of subtlety and guile, "trop bon et trop bête" was certainly not true of him. German officers were often anxious for a little sport, and it was Albert who led them to "achever" a wild boar or a gazelle, or arranged eventful fishing for them. From this he came to be accepted as a "good" Frenchman by the Germans, and it was thus that he found out so much and so regularly about German plans. When I met him he was very nearly at the end of his tether in the dangerous game of duplicity which he was playing, his "cover," as they say in the expressive jargon of secrecy, was all but blown. Yet he continued to go about among Germans even after he was suspected, and did not abandon direct methods of spying until the hunt was up. His poor wife, another of our splendid "Madames," was then haled before the local Gestapo and beaten and interrogated for a day. She knew everything but gave away nothing. She was taken into the woods to show the Germans where we were hiding (she passed very close to me), but she persuaded them that she was a silly ignorant woman and they let her go. To "make sure" in their gross mindless way, they smashed up her house. During this dreadful period Albert was unchanged. He was as full as ever of bold assurances, as full as ever of heroics and boasting defiance. "Death for me," he would say, "is a trifle. Me a prisoner! Never! I would fall in the field of combat, assurez-vous, even if the death-stroke had to be delivered by my own hand." And he meant it too. Our British insularity is most insular in this: we cannot believe that a boastful man can be brave.

After the women, to whom I must give first place, the fraternity of the Gardes de Chasse and Gardes de Forêt (or State Foresters) were the most important foundation of resistance. Not only have I not yet heard of a single case of betrayal by one of these officials, but not even of one case in which they did not give all help no matter what risks were involved.

On the other side of the mountainous barrier north of our town there lived another Garde, whom I like to describe as the companion picture to Albert, so like in his circumstances, so different in his character and method. He was also a hero, but more after our dour British style: strong and absolutely silent. The valley in which he lived was very different to ours. It had its indomitable Madames scattered here and there, its brilliant oases of courage and magnanimity, but a main German supply line ran through it, and so it lived under an even bleaker cloud of oppression than hung over our town: gallantry was deployed and scattered, not "bunched" together as with us. Two of our English officers, one of them gravely wounded,[1] were in hiding in this valley, and the Garde de Forêt acted as a go-between and message-bearer, meeting my colonel and myself at the edge of the wood near his house. As his house was near the road and thus unapproachable in daylight, a further go-between was necessary between us and the forester, and this was provided by an elderly drunkard inhabiting a semi-cave, semi-shack, made of spare bits of corrugated iron. The cave was situated by a farmhouse in the woods. This farmhouse, in turn, was inhabited by an elderly peasant couple, whose terror at the oppression was matched by their incomprehension. The poor, blear-eyed, old grey-beard and his wife, with her black straw hat perched so far forward on her head

---

[1] I refer to Major D. B. Reynolds and Captain A. Whateley Smith, of the 2nd S.A.S. Regt. They were sheltered by M. and Mme. le Rolland of Pierre Percé for two months. Attempting to cross the lines, they were both captured near Raon l'Etape, and barbarously murdered by the Germans at Rotenfels some three weeks later on November, 25th, 1944. They were both greatly loved men.

that to see she was obliged to hold her chin almost parallel to the ground, these two perfect models for some macabre tale by de Maupassant, looked upon us, on the rare occasions when they saw us, with such frantic dread that I am still in doubt as to whether they did not think us Germans. The Garde de Forêt took a practical view of this unfortunate couple. "Steal what you want," he said, "but don't let them see you. They are nervous."

I can see him now, that brave man, coming towards us, with his subtle parade of innocence, his gloomy and yet confident handsome face, and his reserve, which was so very English that in spite of his characteristically French clothes and gestures, those of our men for whom this was a "first visit to France" felt an instant fellow-feeling. He was quite silent on important occasions. We would ask news of the two officers. Without a word he kicked off a clog, worked off the slipper underneath, pulled off the outer sock, then the inner sock, and from between his naked toes drew forth a tiny wedge of paper. The answer was written and put back in the toes, and in a few moments he stood before us fully clothed as if nothing had happened. Then we wanted news about the Germans. Yes, he had some. Tersely, mono-syllabically if possible, he told us. He was like an Englishman in this: that he reflected, without distortion, and without mitigation, all the gloom of any given situation, but somehow, by the very boldness of his acceptance, he sent your spirits up, and not, as you might have expected, down. His silences were truly eloquent.

The old drunkard was always in our conferences if for no other reason than that his crazy habitation was the most convenient rendezvous in this inlet of the valley. He was an "old soldier" in the dictionary and slang senses of that term. In happier days he had been the holder of a distinguished French medal, but in view of his irregularities this had been officially plucked off his breast. He conceived a wild, I think an amorous affection, for my colonel. For some reason he always expressed absolute contempt for us parachutists, holding up our light carbine to special ridicule. "We had a better gun than that," he would say; "something you could hit a man with. And what's the effective range—two hundred metres you say—*Mon Dieu!* I've knocked a man down at seven hundred with our old rifle. And how many wounds have you got Puh! In the war of 'fourteen I was struck eighteen times. And tell me, when you fall in the parachute doesn't it give you the ' baby feeling ' in your stomach? And the landing on the earth? Can that be something? " He would sit chuckling at us from under his straggling yellow grey moustache and through his yellow teeth. He always wore a hat, a smart broad-brimmed trilby of many years ago, while to protect his poor old limbs from the cold he wore two suits, both much battered.

Like his companion picture Albert, the Garde de Forêt was unchanged in liberation. He asked me, when I went to thank him, to come and have lunch with him the following day, an invitation which I, of course, accepted. I can be gluttonous upon occasion, but the six courses of this meal were far beyond my own capacity. I was accompanied by a French friend, Jacques Jay, and I expostulated with him afterwards. "Look here," I said, " this is all wrong. To thank this man, all we can do is to accept a banquet, and from him who fed us miraculously when we were starving." We set about the business of obtaining cigarettes and soap, which were both rarities, from the American army. Three days later I presented them to the Garde de Forêt. "C'est bien gentil, "he said, "c'est *très* gentil," and disappeared into the next room. After a loud bang he came back with an opened bottle of excellent champagne and a huge cake.

But I run ahead of my story. I have said that the woods were kept free of "grey lice" by the courage and inexperience of untrained boys. A few Maquisard groups came out from these woods and fought. There were two of these groups whom I knew well, led by men who provided strange contrasts. Both of them held bases near our town.

One of them was called Joubert. Being a professional soldier he brought a needed calm to the clumsy and temperamental enthusiasm of our remaining Maquis. He was one of those simple, ordinary conscientious men who pass for humdrum in uneventful times, but to whom people gravitate naturally, towards whom they instinctively grope for support, in times of danger. His leadership was based on that kind of authority and was of the simplest character. He kept his band well disciplined, well fed, and made them into a telling striking weapon. He chose his times and places of attack not only with exactness but with psychological effect. When things looked worst he methodically cheered flagging spirits by organising and carrying out an ambuscade. Towards the end of September he was captured in his house in the town where he had come to collect some necessaries. Mercifully the Germans never knew that he was the ambuscadeer who had been plaguing them so long, but they knew that he had much information about us in the woods. The torment used in his case, when he was brought before the Gestapo, was particularly horrible: his feet were battered with a heavy pestle until all the bones of the feet and toes were broken. He knew everything and he told nothing. Thinking about him, I often remember the epitaph on a soldier's grave in Gibraltar: "The soldier," runs the legend, "is like God. In peacetime the people neglect him, in war they call on his aid."

The other leader, a man considerably older than Joubert, was called Etienne. He it was who had been mistaken for an enemy agent at the house of Madame Rossi. He was one of the most villainous-looking men I ever saw. Cruikshanks' drawing of Bill Sikes in his nightcap bears a curiously close resemblance to him. The alarm he caused at Madame Rossi's house was not unnatural, for, in addition to his terrible appearance, like a good Alsatian he spoke French with hideous Germanic gutteral consonants, interspersed with flat little vowels; in fact some knowledge of German was essential to an easy understanding of his French. Add to all this a black cap pulled over his brows and a simian gait, and you have some notion of what this ragamuffinly and courageous man looked like. He led a band as singular as himself and much in the same style. They were all elderly men for their job, the youngest not less than fifty, the oldest well over sixty. They came from heaven knows where, they seemed to be a band of old tramps and beachcombers. Even in the Maquis you could generally guess by some tell-tale remnant of clothing and manner the social stratum from which people came, and these old hobbledehoys had all the appearance of having been drawn from among the very poorest of the poor. They were not a melancholy band, however. They shared a weakness for the bottle with their leader, and on the many occasions when we met they were all alurch in the highest of festal moods.

Through that unending dismal drizzle of rain which afflicts the highlands, they ranged over the whole area of those vast forests, murdering Germans on lonely by-roads or surprising them horribly in houses where they were sheltering. They were puzzling fellows. On one occasion two Algerian Milice agents came to the Maquis disguised as would-be recruits to us. They were made prisoner but escaped. Neither got away: one was ambushed by our men, while the other was chased by Etienne, who shot him. I met him that evening and said I was glad to hear that he had shot this spy, and thanked him. With arms around each other's shoulders for support, the "groupe Etienne" were listening with crazy grins of appreciation to our talk. Etienne appeared very shocked at my remark. He, hurried me aside. "Pas devant les autres," he said gravely "zes incidents zont mal bour la dischipline." What this captain of highwaymen meant at that moment I have never understood. A few more men like Etienne, a few more groups like his, and another Maquis might have been re-formed. As it was, his incessant patrols and ambuscades round the woods further convinced the Germans that they were living precariously in the midst of a huge uprising. And then, one day, Etienne was found dead in the woods. He had succumbed to a sudden stroke. No one ever saw the band of old ragamuffins again. They dispersed, with no stomach for fight without their leader, back to whatever hovels and alleys they had come from.

From all I had heard in England from well-informed people, and from my own experience of Frenchmen, I expected that a major problem in this grisly life of the Maquis would come from the passionate political dissensions which still, apparently, agitated France even during her united resistance. Such was not the case. On the rarest occasions only one heard amid the turmoil of the great struggle the lesser clarion-calls of political loyalties or discord. I remember a foolish French officer dismissing from his command (as though one could "dismiss" people in the middle of a forest) a young man for "incorrect" behaviour, an action inspired chiefly by the fact that the officer was of the extreme right and the young man of the extreme left. I remember also a conversation with a young Maquisard, whose family, so far as he knew, had been exterminated and whose house had been razed, who confided to me that as a Communist he could not altogether resist admiring Hitler as a great proletarian leader whose devotion to his own proletariat had been so remarkable. But these occasions were insignificant. Political speculation, day-dreaming, and even discord, were luxuries of the mind which vanished before the awful demands of that never-ceasing nightmare of life. I only met one man, old Père Joseph, to whom politics remained a vital interest throughout the ordeal.

This strange gnome-like old man, another de Maupassant model, lived in a little farm near our town at the edge of the wood, and as this farm was situated in a fold between hills not visible from the road, it had never been visited by the Germans. Père Joseph—his title was merely a tribute to his age—allowed us to use his barn as a shelter from time to time when the rigours of the rain-drenched forest became intolerable. He kept two cows and some pigs, with whom he shared his food, which, as he ate it out of a pot-de-chambre, he would declare to be adequate for his needs. "Like all really good farmers," he would add, "I feed my animals very well." When his wife was alive, he once explained, they used to eat very fine potages, but since her death he had not found the time or the energy to bestir himself in the kitchen, and so he nourished himself on a basis of equality with his beasts. As he sat in his rough peasant's clothes and clogs, with a napkin tied round his head, and puffing through his immense protruding moustache, he looked astonishingly like a drawing by Daumier. He was a Communist. "Churchill," he would mumble, "il est bien. De Gaulle—bien. But," he would hold up a finger, "it is to be remarked that it was after Churchill had visited Moscow that the tide of victory turned. Stalin—that is the one. Ah, Stalin—he is the great man. Dommage que Churchill n'est pu' communiste." I do not think that his brand of Communism, for all its passion, would have recommended him to the orthodox schools of his cult. I asked him once how he reconciled his Communist conscience with the plain fact that he was a proprietor, for apart from his pigs and cows he had a sizeable orchard of fruit trees. "Ma foi," he cried in vexation, "all my life I have worked to acquire what you see! All my life! In the Communist state it would be mine from birth and without toil, and very much larger too. Mon Dieu!"

Among our Maquisards were two Russian escaped prisoners of war, great clumsy biscuit-faced men. They could speak a little, a very little, German, and practically no French at all. I really doubt whether they ever in the least understood into what galère they had fallen in those disastrous Vosges. Their minds were like those of very small children. The simplest necessities, on which their survival depended, had to be explained to them with the utmost care. I once found them at night sitting together smoking on a bridge on the main road. By luck no German had passed or noticed them. When I had stamped out their cigarettes, cursed them in bad German, and got them on their way to the forest, one of them came back to me. He said, "Papirosa—teuer—kharasho," meaning, "Cigarette, expensive, good." I think he construed my anger as formal disapproval of smoking. They knew about discipline but about precious little else. It would have been well if we had had a sharp-tongued maternally-minded woman to look after these unfortunates. (We did have such a one for a very brief moment, but she seems to have been a German agent provocateur, so it did not much signify.) There were many such lost souls wandering about France in those days. To my great inconvenience, both physically and morally, the two Russians attached themselves to me in the conviction that I knew Russian. The fact that a knowledge of French was rare among us Englishmen, and that I could talk French passably well, had probably given them the idea that I had the "gift of tongues" and could switch on to any idiom with equal ease. Whatever the explanation, these unlucky castaways always came to me with their grievances, so that we whiled away many an hour together as they poured forth their tales in the, to me, incomprehensible and musical language of Russia, and I replied in Persian in the hope that the occasional Russian words in that language might convey some meaning to them. It never did, though I rose in esteem as a linguist all round. By a process of evolution, a kind of German, composed exclusively of nouns and gestures, was established as our channel of communication.

Père Joseph was not a man of facile enthusiasms. His normal outlook was one of gloom, a wide comprehensive gloom. He deplored the conduct of his country and his country's Allies, with the exception of Russia, and even

when we gave him a treat one night in the form of an
excellent rice pudding with cream he could give no better
token of approval than "Military Rations. All right for
soldiers, I suppose." But one night we took shelter in his
barn with a party which included the two Russians, and
when I introduced them in the morning his old lined face
fairly wrinkled with pleasure. He adjusted his tin
spectacles and swept up his moustache. "Ah vous!" he
cried. "Soldiers of the Red Army. That's good. Com-
munists! That's good!' And he shook them both warmly
by the hand. I conveyed to them that he was pleased to
meet them, as he was a Communist like them. But here
an unfortunate sequel followed. They both shook their
heads, while the less incoherent of the twain said:
"Communistichiski—in armée—nicht gut." It was a
blow, and I am glad that I had the chivalry not to
celebrate any triumph of capitalism over our long-
suffering and far-from-welcoming host. Poor Père
Joseph! He never liked us, and bitter necessity made us
use his hospitality as much as we could. In the end the
Germans did visit his home, and he was taken away to
die miserably in some foul concentration camp. He also
knew enough to destroy us, and he also said nothing.

Perhaps, for the sake of clarity, I may now briefly say
something about ourselves. Our original aim in coming
to these forests was to establish ourselves in a Germanless
area where we could receive our heavy weapons and
further reinforcements. The area around this town, in
which Germans were occasionally stationed, and to which
they put out occasional patrols, this intermittently
haunted place, had to do, and, thanks to that shining
loyalty of the people, it did do very well. During the
ten days of mid-September we received our jeeps, "les
Jims" as the French called them, with their heavy
machine-guns, and most of our reinforcements, all by
parachute. Then at last we could go over to an attacking
rôle. Our aim was to make widely dispersed attacks on
German convoys, to pose as a forward thrust of the main

army, to cause panic and disorganisation among the Germans, and thus ease the task of the American Army in their advance to the Rhine. This plan was also doomed to failure. Owing to the small number of roads in these Vosgian glens, "jeeping attacks" could only be maintained for a short time. A major supply problem, following on their rapid advance to the Moselle, had arisen for the Allied Armies, and this was to delay their attack till the winter.

Of this we knew nothing. Liaison between the different Intelligence branches was markedly imperfect, and in consequence we got instructions to prepare for an advance which had, in fact, been cancelled. (I do not wish to seem as though I am airing a grievance. In campaigns of the magnitude of the second battle of France, such relatively minor breakdowns of staff machinery are bound to occur somewhere.) After some ten days of effective offensive violence (taking us to the end of September) our position was compromised, and we were gradually reduced again to ambuscading on foot from the woods. We had the consolation of knowing that we had hurt the enemy, and compelled them to withdraw considerable numbers of troops from their front line on the Moselle in order to counter-attack their invisible foes in the Vosges. Now let me return to my subject.

In nothing was the spirit of our town more plainly or more dangerously shown than in their conduct during what became known as "les parachutages" and "les droppages,"[1] when from the air we received our heavy weapons and reinforcements in the fields sloping up from the town's edge to the forests and mountains. We aimed at secrecy but obtained demonstrations. On the first of these occasions we had issued forth from our rocky fastness in the utmost of hugger-mugger, taking a few volunteers from the Maquis and from the townsfolk, as we needed to work with all speed and as many hands as

[1]The interchange of words was well illustrated here. The correct English term is a "drop," but in France our men invariably referred to "parachutarges" and "droppidges." "Drop" became quite obsolete.

we could, so that there should be no tell-tale sign in the morning. But the news was whispered abroad, and by the second or third "droppage," in spite of all we could do to prevent it, for the Germans were hardly a mile away, the entire population turned out. Imagine a nocturnal race-meeting at Newmarket, imagine a crowd streaming across the heath to a moonlight Two Thousand Guineas, and you have a fair idea of what one of these "droppages" behind the enemy lines looked like. It still seems to me that in nothing were we more fortunate than in this: that the Germans were never attracted by the hullabaloo to mount a large night attack against us on one of these occasions. Perhaps they were too puzzled by the whole business, which was indeed surprising in the highest degree.

Parachuting nights opened according to plan, as a rule. Our men and the Maquis cautiously marched by roundabout paths to stations at the sides of copses, where in moonlight whole companies of men were invisible. The fun usually began towards midnight when the Groupe Etienne arrived, always very bright with drink and bringing some bottles of hideous raw spirit as a protection against cold. Their songs and their yells of welcome to us and their French comrades set a new tone for the rest of the night. There was nothing to do about it. If we had tried to prevent them coming they would have come just the same, and when I once told Etienne that the noise *must* stop forthwith, he cordially agreed, and, putting his hands to his mouth, fairly bellowed across the field: "Silence! Tais toi! Un beu de dischipline ou je t'schlage." He was answered with a cheer. But, indeed, towards the hour of the arrival of 'planes the rowdiness of this group was lost in the general hubbub of the thickening crowd. The curious facility of secret intelligence which all Frenchmen developed during the war allowed the entire population to know with more or less precision the hour of the great event, and, as it drew near, so they began to swarm out into the field. I do not pretend that everyone came in a spirit of altruistic patriotism; there was loot to be had, particularly tempting loot in the cigarettes and boots in the packages, and for the women, who attended these meetings in increasing numbers, very great temptations in the silken parachutes. The remarkable thing is that they did not take more in the confusion of collection.

The dramatic moment was when the distant hum of an aeroplane could be heard. As the sound of the nearing machine increased, a hush would descend on the field while the signallers flashed the torches. As a rule, the aeroplane would circle once over the field and then retire for the "run-in." All this while there was the silence of expectancy over the field. Then the aeroplane would come back, lower now, for the "drop." One would see its silhouette, suddenly accompanied by and then leaving little floating round black objects, as though a great black planet were escaping from its moons, and then in rapid crescendo the hubbub would mount again in volume. "Ce sont des hommes." "Ce sont des *containeurs*." "C'est un Jim." Swiftly coming down at steep angles, the black objects resolved themselves into the shapes of parachuting men, parachuted containers, and a great hanging constellation of four meant that a Jeep was descending by seeming slow stages. The excitement of the crowd was now tremendous and, as with the splintering crashes of branches, with resounding clatters on rooftops, the lurching cracks of the Jeep crates, or a thump on the ground, the humans, weapons and transport landed in and a-straddle the field, dark clouds of scurrying humanity would dash to landed parachutes, while calls and shouts echoed on all hands. "Mon Colonel," I can hear Etienne's great roar from within the woods, "il y a izi un Jim suspendu tans les arbres!"

The excitement of one drop was hardly begun before a second machine could be heard nearing. The same performance was repeated, but in more confusion, as the events overlapped. By the fifth or sixth drop the scene of chaos was formidable. Lurching, struggling groups zig-zagged like ambitious ants up the hill, carrying containers to the edge of the forest. Search-parties plunged through thickets looking for missing men, while —really how strange that the Germans never did come out—resounding mighty blows of hammers on the crates sent forth loud echoes up and down our sleeping valley. Exhaustion kills discretion, and as the night wore on, as we staggered along with our third or fourth container, voices grew louder, torches were more carelessly shone hither and thither, and the Groupe Etienne would shout to each other in the dark even more boldly than their wont. On "Jeep nights" the episode concluded by piling all material on to the transports and driving them through the town and up into our brigandish home. Often on the way back a door would be opened in the town by a woman offering us a hot meal. I do not think that any one could have lived there and not known about the "droppages." They all knew and no one gave us away.

Shortly after the final reception of Jeeps there occurred a strange episode, one of the strangest of which I heard during the war, which should also be told to the honour of that town in the Vosges. Our plan was to lay ambushes at some distance from our centre, never in our valley, but in the valleys adjoining it, or on the other side of the ranges. The closest ambush point was about two miles from where we were hidden. It was here that this strange event took place.

The Germans had taken all motor transport from the French and even most of their bicycles. A bicyclist on the road might or might not be a German, the chances were in favour of the German, but every car was certainly German. We gave instructions to the ambush parties that all cars were to be attacked, as all cars were German. In ambush of this kind, done from Jeeps, you can pick and choose only on the rarest occasions, as you are nearly always visible at the last moment to the approaching vehicle. The ambush where this episode occurred, that nearest to the town, was of such a kind.

Now the information on which our instructions were based was accurate, but not, as it turned out, absolutely so. There was one exception to this generalisation, only one, and that concerned one of our main protectors, the Mayor, who alone had been allowed to keep his car. He so rarely used his car that this exception had been rather easily overlooked. He had an electric brougham. By the unluckiest and unlikeliest chance in the world the Mayor took it into his head to go for a drive in his brougham on the same afternoon as our ambush was mounted, and by a further million-to-one chance he set out just as the Jeeps moved into position. The electric brougham was the first car to drive down that fatal road. . . . It sped on, at its modest speed, it turned a corner—it received the full charge of eight heavy machine-guns. The brougham disintegrated, ceased to exist, fell in pieces, but by a miracle the Mayor was not touched, and succeeded in rolling out and over the road into the ditch. When he could collect his thoughts he realised by whom he had been attacked. He took out his pocket handkerchief and waved it as a sign. We could not take prisoners then, and on the Mayor's hand the fire of eight guns was instantly directed, but he was again not touched. He crawled back home along the ditch.

Albert came and told my Colonel about this ghastly episode in the evening. We had not heard about it before as we had been on the other side of the forest. We were much perturbed; he and I and Albert stood a while speechless in the deepening twilight among the crags, while the fir trees dripped and the Maquisard cooks were preparing the nauseating evening meal behind us. Albert explained in full. He filled in a comprehensive picture, depicting every grisly detail, and laying pedantic stress on every possible unfortunate consequence. Our conference was interrupted by a hiss from the sentry. We took cover behind trees, holding our carbines ready, and looked down the steep torrent bed which led to our fastness. A figure carrying a burden was just visible in the gloom plodding up towards us by the rough path. Presently Albert whispered from behind his tree: "All right. I know him. I'll go down." We covered Albert as he went down to our mysterious visitor. We saw them meet, saw them talking together, and presently Albert motioned him to ascend. He was a messenger from the Mayor. He brought us two bottles of champagne and the following note: "Remerciements pour la salve tirée en mon honneur cet après midi."

The unhesitating loyalty of the people of this town was all the more remarkable as right at the beginning of our operations the Germans had discovered that they had given help to parachutists. On the 18th of August, a month before the time I describe, the Gestapo had paraded all the men of the town in front of the school, marched them to Gestapo Headquarters about two miles distant, and there interrogated them. They had kept a few prisoners, and sent back the remainder with a severe warning. On the 24th of September, a few days after the incident of the ambush just related, the people had to pay the price for their courage, and for rashness, of which we also must bear some part of the blame. The men, numbering some two hundred and ten, were again paraded in front of the school. The Gestapo Commandant harangued them. He said that the Germans knew that there were parachutists in the region, that the most severe punishment was in consequence to be meted out to the men of the town as a warning to other French towns and as a retribution on this community. He told them that no mercy would be shown and that they were destined for concentration camps. "But we will," he concluded, "allow one generous exception. If any man will come forward now with information about the parachutists he will be given his liberty." They all knew exactly where we were hidden in the forest. The German repeated his offer. Not one man moved.

They were marched off, as before, to Gestapo Head-quarters. From there they were sent to those unspeakable prison camps whose like had not been seen before in the history of civilised man. Of these two hundred and ten, one hundred and forty never returned. The offer of liberty was repeated to them later, privily, under more tempting circumstances. There is no evidence that they ever gave us away, indeed there is evidence that every one of these men remained steadfast to the end. The evidence is strong. I visited our hiding-place after the war and I found many traces of ourselves, but none of a German ever having been there. (I know how to trace Germans; I have done it often.) Even after this blow to our Allies, we were still able to keep up the attack, and that made me suppose then that the loyalty with which we were surrounded was of the sublime character which can resist torture. Time has made this into a conviction.

I have not the command of language to express the admiration I feel.

In the first half of October our own adventures came to an end. We had succeeded, with the Maquis, in spreading panic among the Germans, but without a major Allied attack following, the Germans could take our measure and concentrate their counter-attack on us. All the roads, including the forest paths, were now heavily patrolled; there could be no more jeeping. All the parachuting grounds were strongly picketed. We were reduced to small-scale ambuscades once more, but we were fast running out of food and ammunition. Winter came early that year, and the first weeks of October were cold. We left our town for a last attack in the valley over the mountains to the north, and congregated in the forests surrounding an obscure forester's house in the centre of the dividing ranges. It was there that we received instructions by wireless to cross the enemy lines[1] to the American Seventh Army, but before we left we saw one more example of what French loyalty means.

A month or so previous to mid-October the family of a Garde de Forêt who lived here (not to be confused with him previously mentioned) had sheltered some of our men and Maquisards who accompanied them. The Germans had discovered this and organised reprisals. When we arrived one of us went to the house to ask for food. He found a terrified young woman, the wife of the forester, who said that the Germans had been to take away her husband, that they had not found him, that they had said they would come back on the Monday (the next day), and if they did not find the husband they would burn down the house. She could not help, she said. The poor girl had an elderly mother and a small child. She spoke with such wild terror that it was difficult to know whether she was imagining more than she knew.

It was pouring with rain. Sleeping out had become unbearable even to the toughest of the tough. We sheltered in the sawmill adjoining the house and helped ourselves to the family's store of apples. In the morning a few of us paid a last visit to the other Garde de Forêt— the silent man in the Northern valley whom I have already mentioned—in order to get some supplies of food to last us for the few days necessary to cross the lines. When we came back we found a horrible tragedy.

Late in the afternoon the Gestapo had come as they said they would. There were five of them. They questioned the family closely, not only as to the whereabouts of the husband but as to the whereabouts of the parachutists. Then they turned the family out and rounded up their chickens, which they put in one of their cars. They then burnt down the house and the mill, and turned the girl,

[1] Of the ninety-two British officers and men who took part in this operation, three were killed in battle and twenty-nine taken prisoner, most of the latter in the crossing of the enemy lines. With one exception all the prisoners were murdered several weeks after capture.

the old mother and the baby on to the road. Then they left
after them. During all this time our men were in the
forests surrounding the house. With the greatest ease
they could have killed the five Gestapo, and might, with
luck, have saved the family—for the moment. But we
could not take an old woman and a child with us in our
then desperate condition. There was also an ugly likeli-
hood that at the first sound of a shot the Gestapo would
kill the family immediately, suspecting a pre-arranged
ambuscade. Five Gestapo men would be a prize—but not
enough at the cost. We owed too much to this family.
So in the bitterness of frustration, and to the rage of the
men, until the matter was explained to them from group
to group, the officer in charge gave the order to hold fire.
We were condemned to show gratitude in a sickeningly
obscure fashion. But the marvel of the incident appears
if it is considered from the other angle, from the point
of view of that family facing privation, and the loss of
what might remain of accustomed happiness. They knew,
all French people knew, that information about parachutists could buy exceptional favours; nor was there
much danger of our men, even as eye-witnesses, discovering treachery. How easy to whisper a word apart to one
of these men and save all, nor lose reputation in so doing.
How easy! But that word was not whispered; instead,
they sat by and saw everything they loved and possessed
smashed to pieces, stolen, or destroyed by fire. They were
last seen walking down the road towards the Northern
valley, in the pouring rain, weeping bitterly. They were
turned on to the road as beggars. They were the last
French people any of us saw before reaching the American
Army.

About six weeks later I returned to the Vosges in order
to start inquiries about the men whom we had lost there
and of whom there was as yet no trace. The event which
had seemed so imminent to us in September and so
remote in October had actually occurred a short time

before, at the end of November. The American Army had crossed the Meurthe and the Germans had fled from all these valleys. I can find no better description of the sensation of being freed than that given by Miss Gertrude Stein, who was herself in a French town when it was liberated. "You feel natural," she says. "You may feel good or you may feel bad, but you feel natural." At last we were all natural again. It was wonderful simply to stand in a street in broad daylight. I must confess that it was with some feeling of trepidation that I returned to our town: so much had been suffered, and so much of it for our unworthy sake. But their loyalty was without stint. I was acclaimed as if I had saved the world. We had become a legend. Prodigies of valour were ascribed to me personally, to which, in truth, I can make not the smallest shadow of a claim. I do not wish to exaggerate the generosity of these people or to sentimentalise; I only write down what I saw happen.

It was during this second visit that I learned of the very extraordinary manner in which this fine resistance had first been organised, of the distant origin of much of this spirit of valour, and the more I think of it the more deeply am I impressed at the way unnoticed things can resolve great events.

I heard from our friends, as we spoke in the new luxury of free speech, that the man to whom most was owed was one who had never appeared to us, nor of whom we had ever heard—the parish priest. Throughout the war, they said, it was he who had kept the spirit of loyalty and patriotism alive, it was he who had first organised a Maquis here at the very beginning of resistance, who had built a system which he then joined to the main one for the escape of "baled-out" airmen and of fugitive prisoners of war. "Without him," said Madame Rossi, and her evidence counted for a lot with me, "things might have been very different here." It became clear why we had not heard of him. As the Germans kept so close a watch on him, more close than on any other man, his least abnormal movement was likely to be discovered. He posed as a neutral, and maintained contact with the resistance only through a very few people and at well-disguised meetings. These few were sworn to absolute secrecy. In the midst of the many secrets of the town his was the most thoroughly guarded. My anxiety to meet him was great.

I found a man whose appearance suggested immediately one of those pre-Reformation clerics whose zeal for their holy calling was only matched by their fearful prowess on the field of battle. A stern, lean, cadaverous appearance, wonderfully made gentle by the humour and grace of his smile. There was a pleasant irony in the way he spoke; you somehow felt from his expressions that while as a priest, without any easy hope of success, he considered himself charged with the machinery of redemption, as a man he was left in blank wonder at the heights and the depths of human nature which he had witnessed. We had some business to discuss together. He was waging a campaign against the counter-atrocities which had inevitably begun to appear all over France; he knew where some of our lost men had been murdered, buried, or taken away, and he wanted to know from me where the bodies of the two Algerian spies were to be found. "The dead must be respectfully buried," he said grimly; "a point which my parishioners may sometimes ignore." He told me about the origins of the Maquis and of the absurd political rivalries which were already showing themselves in claims for deeds of courage. Sometimes, when a point amused him—and he had much sense of humour—he emphasised a remark with the subtlest exaggeration of a priestly gesture. A grand man.

At the end of our first discussion together I told him that I wanted to thank him for all that he had done for us, but that there was nothing I could say that was not absurdly inadequate. I said that if there was something we could do to show our gratitude, I was certain we would do it if it was in the least within the bounds of possibility.

He was silent in thought for a moment, and then: "As regards me, there is no question of your owing gratitude," he said, and added enigmatically: "You know I would do anything for the English."

"That is kind." I waited in silence for another reply which I felt him to be forming in his mind.

"You see," he said, "speaking for myself, not for the town, the debt was on my side, and I am only happy to have discharged it. I have only once been to England, and it was there that I was made your debtor. . . ." He then told me an extraordinary story.

At the beginning of the war this priest was a chaplain in the French Army, and when the disaster of 1940 occurred his regiment was among those who were evacuated by us from Dunkirk. For the first time, then, he met Englishmen in large numbers, and he saw to his amazement that the legendary "flegme britannique" was no legend at all. The calm and the patience on the beaches made him wonder whether, perhaps, all was lost indeed. He told me that he waded to his boat behind an English private soldier during a severe raid by German aircraft; that as they waited their turn in the water, the English soldier lit his pipe and cursed in vexation because it took him so long to get a steady flame. But it was after his arrival in England that the priest contracted that great debt to discharge which he felt his personal honour deeply engaged. The problem of how to accommodate the many foreign troops who suddenly arrived in England was difficult; the priest was sent with several other Frenchmen to a small hotel in a town on the South Coast. The town was bombed several times while he was there. He told me that never in his life had he suffered such appalling depression of spirits, such despair, such grief, as at this time, though, unlike many other Frenchmen then, he was not assailed by any doubts as to where his duty lay: it lay with his parishioners in the Vosges. But what wretched humiliation was he not

likely to find there? Heavily and insistently the bitterness
of defeat weighed on his mind and soul.

The hotel where they stayed was kept by two women.
It was a good hotel. These two women devised what they
could to cheer the Frenchmen who had been billeted on
them. They taught them English words, they learned
French words in return, they explained the news in the
papers to them, they borrowed a wireless so that they
could listen to those first French programmes of
the Gaullist movement. But what impressed my friend
most was that in spite of the danger, the terrors, the
bombing, the life of the hotel went on as smoothly and
quietly as though this were a holiday season in peace.
The routine, the meals, the style of comfort went on
uninterrupted. It was this simple fact which made the
deepest impression on him. It is easy to laugh at English
seaside hotels, but this one achieved something that can
well be called great.

"It was those two women," said Monsieur le Curé
with a sudden burst of enthusiasm, "who proved to me
that the English are very formidable people. I recognised
in a flash we must be formidable too, and that it was
possible, above all, that it was possible."

That was his story, and that was one of the origins of
a resistance to which I would like to pay some homage
which is not too unworthy.

When I thought over this extraordinary, this utterly
unexpected story, my mind worked back to another
incident: another tale of Anglo-French accord.

Some years before the war, in the interests of Anglo-
French understanding, a body of men interested in
exchanges of our two cultures organised an exhibition in
London of some positively incomprehensibly advanced
works of art. A large fashionable crowd congregated in
a gallery, and proceedings were opened by an English
professor, who explained the aims of the French, English,
and other artists concerned. He told us that this group
of men "had not a shred of respect" for the traditions of

European civilisation, that they were "out" to "smash" its insupportable "humbug, dross, and hypocritical conventions," by which he seemed to indicate any behaviour or belief noticeably different from that of an early ape-man gibbering in a cave. I forget the rest of what he said, but if any one had reflected for a moment, he or she might have noticed that, with very little editing and a change of scenery, the speech of this mild, foolish, over-educated, empty-headed man might have been delivered to different plaudits with a large black swastika bound to the speaker's right arm. He was followed by a Frenchman, who, speaking with that unendurable arrogance of which only certain French intellectuals hold the secret, gave us a further and more detailed catalogue of features of our Western World which he and his associates hoped shortly to "smash," and which most of the men and women in his audience, and he himself for all I know, were shortly to spend five and a half weary years in defending. All this and the scoriæ on the walls were received with long faces of impressed approval, or with the well-simulated enthusiasm of the modish. To my shame I remember myself murmuring, with pretended excitement, some bosh of the period in praise.

Exactly how this manifestation of Germanic excess and indecency was supposed to draw us closer to the fine restrained genius of France was not explained in the programme or by the quality of the exhibits, but such was the declared aim of the organisers.

I could not help comparing this elaborate and fatuously painstaking attempt at mutual inspiration with what those two women of the South Coast town hotel did a few years later. Acting, without self-consciousness, for the best, they had achieved—well, what had they not achieved? Was our operation really so very unsuccessful? It has not yet been explained why the Germans did not remain to fight in those easily defendable valleys. Is it possible that they *still* felt too uncertain of their position, *still* believed in a vast hidden

host waiting for the sign to rise in all their thousands?
But even if this supposition is not admissible, it can be
said, without any exaggeration at all, that those two
women set in motion the most formidable chain of
events. They caused panic to the enemies of France in
a whole province, they dislocated German military dispositions in a whole sector of the front line, they raised
an army in the defence of all that makes human life
honourable and endurable, and they inspired a loyalty
and love which, with the debasement of the term
"Charity," is hard to describe; we have now no fine
enough word to depict such virtue.

I made one more visit to the Vosges, nearly a year
after our "drop" and nearly nine months after the
liberation. We had been invited to send a guard of
honour to the memorial service for the townsmen who
had perished in the concentration camps, and we took
the occasion to form a military cemetery for those of
our men who had been killed in battle or been murdered
by the Germans in the valleys of the Vosges highlands.
It was characteristic of the generosity of this sorely
oppressed place that they should have asked us to provide
a guard and felt honoured to bury our dead among their
own. I repeat again that had it not been that they helped
us as they did, or had we not been there to be so helped,
most of their tragedies would have been avoided.

It was now, during this last visit, that the extent of the
havoc wreaked on this place became at last clear. Final
hopes were flickering to darkness, for the first time plain
evidence revealed the extent of the ruin. The hundred
and forty men who had died came from a population not
greater than fourteen hundred in all. Similar dreadful
gaps had been made in the populations of all the surrounding villages and towns, but nowhere had such
destruction of human life been wrought as here. In the
precise and terrible logic of Catholic custom, a requiem
mass was offered for every victim in his home town.

Monsieur le Curé estimated that this pious duty would occupy the clergy for the greater part of the coming year. My latest recollection of that place is of streets peopled by black-clothed figures trooping to parish churches, of masses where the simplicity of the ritual was often obscured by the fantasies of local practice, and of the sublime majesty of the "Dies Iræ," the old rude hymn contrasting pathetically with the children's voices.

The inquiry to establish the fate of our missing men was still continuing near by in Germany, and to help in this I interviewed some survivors of the camps. This experience always affected me in the same way: I felt as though I were entering a world whose proportions, colours, action and spring were absolutely unfamiliar, as though by withdrawing every vestige of what is gracious or good you produced a new colour of darkness, profound with mysterious poverty. Nearly always one found oneself wading in unfamiliarly deep psychological waters, and nearly always one could just keep track of the way by gleams of splendid character piercing the blackness with an unearthly light. One of our men who vanished into that vile obscurity is traced by a single incident. He was lying on a straw mattress, exhausted after torture, when a woman prisoner, whom he had never seen before, was thrust into the cell and he immediately gave her his bed and lay on the stone floor. Identifications were usually done from photographs. One of these showed the subject with a pleasant smile on his face. He was a prisoner in three camps in succession before he was murdered. He was identified by a Frenchman, among others, who had been his fellow-prisoner in the place where he was killed, and as he looked at the photograph he said these words: "C'est lui, c'est bien lui, c'est bien son charmant sourire." This boy had refused to salute any single one of his Gestapo captors. In their odious childish way the Germans were particularly infuriated by this, and wreaked vengeance on him by daily, hideous, and insane corporal punishments over a period of seven weeks. This Frenchman had seen him at the end, a few days before he was murdered; seen him with his charming smile. I wish it were possible to write something worthy of such things. The wish, I think, is vain. Certain facts and deeds are so made up in themselves of poetry that they become untranslatable.

This incident was not isolated, it was often from such lovely fragments, from a cheering word which was remembered, that the evidence of the grim story was set together.

I learned of the strange processes by which some men could render themselves immune from the corruption of torture. One such man, who had undergone the horrors of the camps, I met about this time in connection with the same inquiry, in Paris. He had the appearance of a man painted by El Greco. He spoke of his sufferings with scientific detachment, one would have said with repulsive detachment, had it not been for the contradicting glow in his eyes. I had learned before I met him that many of his friends in Paris had found themselves exasperated by his impersonal view of what he had witnessed, and by his impersonally moderate attitude towards the Germans, although they knew that he had performed prodigies for our cause before capture, and prodigies of discretion during his imprisonment.

Some explanation of the proud aloofness with which he underwent his ordeals was perhaps to be found in the self-conscious aristocratic traditions of his family, but his own explanation, which he gave to a friend of mine, was at the same time more mechanical and more mysterious. He survived, he said, by means of nothing more recondite than the application of religious devotions to his state. He began with the immense advantage of being an ardent Christian of a traditional kind, he was not in the smallest worried by the grievous trials to reason which the Church still imposes on the faithful, although he was 'a man of a keen, logical mind, just such a one to whom these trials are least tolerable.

This happy accident of soul and temper allowed him to use his religion to the full. He told my friend that he lived a kind of double life in prison: two lives closely united in a system which he devised without difficulty (though the performance was difficult), from the orthodox practice which he knew. He resisted torture, he said, by offering it to God, but to maintain the personal nature of his penance he added to his pain. Thus when obliged to sleep in a cell without bed or blanket he deprived himself of his coat also; when whipped or submitted to other pain he would afterwards lie on stones, in a hateful posture, or he would inflict additional pain on himself with his nails or teeth. To any one who has studied the lives of the saints this manner of mortification is familiar, but in the light of what this saint of our own times told of his experiences, one may doubt whether the approved explanations have always been correct. He had no childish intention of presenting a voracious God of sacrifices with a bumper record of anguish undergone. He followed this system, he said, simply to preserve a sense of his own personality and with that his sanity, and by this means to be able to remain in his state of constant prayer.

I heard of a similar triumph over suffering, that of a distinguished artist,[1] who was imprisoned for a long time in the concentration camps. His experience, in contrast to the foregoing one, was of a more pagan kind. He preserved his sanity by an immense mental effort of concentration on his art. In his mind he worked out the design of a picture, first in general lines and then in detail. Having done this, he imagined to himself a blank canvas, a virgin palette, the paints and brushes which he required, the angle to the window at which he should work, and so on, exactly as if he were at home in his studio. Then through many months he imagined

[1] I withhold the names of both these men, as I do not know whether they wish to be publicly associated with these intimate experiences. I have no hesitation in recording accounts of their experiences as they are of such general and illuminating significance.

the act of painting; he imagined not only the result of such and such application of paint, but followed every individual stroke which he would require, with so perfect an act of fancy that he felt tired or "played out" exactly when he would have done if he had been really painting, not merely thinking about painting in the corner of a filthy hut. His sense of triumph on the completion of this non-existent work was so invigorating, that he was left with a strong determination which he felt that all the cruelty in the world could not smother: to live, to paint his picture. Well, he lived. And then an expectable but curious thing happened. He found he could not paint this picture with which he had lived so long: he had painted it already! Instead, he painted a self-portrait, which, when I saw it, I thought was one of the most beautiful modern portraits I have ever seen. It may have been my imagination, but I thought I detected something of the same Grecoesque look in the portrait that I had seen in that other survivor.

By such rare illuminations as these it was possible to grope from the ordinary world into an abyss of lunatic cruelty, of which, let it be hoped, those innumerable mourners threading their way through French streets to parish churches had an inadequate idea. The illuminations, those "hidden wonders in the human breast," take a prominent place in any recollection of these things, for without them little if anything would be visible; but it would be a foolish error to suppose that they were in the least usual. Indeed, it would be a detestable paradox if it were found that the fruits of such evil as warfare and persecution were good. By-products of anything whatever may be good, but the products of evil are very evil.

I am astonished that in an age which has seen the aftermaths of two wars that satirical parable, "The Dreadful Dragon of Hay Hill," is not one of the most famous in the world. There in deceptively gentle terms the greatest virtues and follies of mankind are laid bare: the loyalty and unselfishness of danger and the remorseless reaction to our best qualities which we allow and even encourage in ourselves when the danger is passed. Can there be any solution of this recurring and fatal predicament in human nature? The parable ends on a note of pessimism, and perhaps that is the right and only answer. Anyone born before 1914 knows the arguments concerning the loyalty engendered by war and the petty discords of peace, knows the anxiety to prolong the loyalty in order to resolve the discords, knows that the most ardent advocates of this desirable consummation have no hope whatsoever of its possibility. We should grow accustomed to the fact that the virtues of war, with few exceptions, grow out of vileness and vanish with the vileness. To have left the Vosges united in a splendid resolve, to have had one's life in those loyal hands and to return to find faction, to find the hands rising hatefully against one another, was a bitter thing to see and contemplate aloof. Men who had fought together now denounced one another, every national disaster was imputed to a local treachery, the tremendous fall of France was assumed to have been a consequence of petty intrigue.

It would be as inept as ungracious for an Englishman to lecture France on the resumption of her most poisonous political traditions at the same time as our own country joyfully celebrated the victory of freedom by renewing her most unintelligent ones; both our countries have one error of reasoning in common: a belief that freedom is much honoured by organised mutual loathing. Englishmen and Frenchmen become embroiled in or detached from this predicament in parallel circumstances. Let me not, therefore, be accused of pompous sermonising if I ask Frenchmen who may read this to recollect how little the element of treachery needed to be calculated in the days when our lives depended on loyalty, and how ignoble, in comparison with that fact, is the present prying into the possible implications of past weakness.

Let me conclude by quoting the testimony of a

Frenchman. The circumstances surrounding the death in battle of one of our officers were obscure, and to obtain some evidence on this subject I visited the doctor of a near-by town, who, I had been told, had helped him secretly at the time of the campaign. I imagine that Marshal Foch was not dissimilar from this short, violent, gaitered doctor: his every expression was accompanied by an equally emphatic gesture in which his black-booted feet and gaitered legs played almost as strong a part as his delicate vivacious hands. I was glad that he was friendly to my regiment, for it seemed clear that his animosities were numerous, strong and sincere. He told me all that I needed to know, and then, for the sake of the man we had both known, he asked me to sit down with him and drink a glass of mirabelle. He had condemned so freely and fiercely in our previous talk that I almost avoided raising the subject of "denunciation," which was at that time much besetting my mind. But when in the glow of sentiment engendered by the occasion and his good liqueur I did say how much I deplored the current fashion of recrimination, he slammed down his glass on the table and stood Napoleonically by the stove. Had he been less Napoleonic he might have looked absurd. As it was, he looked imposing. "That," he said, "is part of a disease." He thrust a cigarette at me and took one of my own. "The peasants, the workmen, the doctors, the officials, they are all afflicted. The peasants will not till, the workmen will not work, and the same with them all. It is a disease. A disease of the mind, mark you. La Victoire!" He drew in a long breath of smoke and slowly whistled it out again, and then paused self-consciously before demolishing the apparent illogicality of his reply. "The cause?" he said. "Simple. People will not realise that the sufferings of war originate in stupidity. Wars begin because we are stupid, they are protracted because we are stupid, and at the end of them we are left with shame at our stupidity. It is simple, but we do not like it. We prefer denunciation."

When I left him the title of a book, the best title, I have always thought, of any book written, kept repeating itself in my mind, *Grandeurs et Misères d'une Victoire*. Hope was not easy to feel then in those mourning valleys, but it were foolish to forget the audacity which had so marvellously sprung up there, spurned though it might be now because it had won only a freedom to mourn; it were equally foolish to forget the clear French spirit which had the courage to analyse, and from that, to overcome, the great grief which oppressed it.

THE END